The Librarian's Guide to Partnerships

Edited by Sherry Lynch

Contributing Editors
Shirley Amore
Jerrie Bethel

Highsmith Press Handbook Series

PRESS

Fort Atkinson, Wisconsin

Published by Highsmith Press LLC
W5527 Highway 106
P.O. Box 800
Fort Atkinson, Wisconsin 53538-0800
1-800-558-2110

The paper used in this publication meets the minimum requirements of
American National Standard for Information Science —
Permanence of Paper for Printed Library Material. ANSI/NISO Z39.48-1992.

Library of Congress Cataloging-in-Publication Data
    The librarian's guide to partnerships / edited by Sherry Lynch.
        p.   cm. -- (Highsmith Press handbook series)
    Includes index.
    ISBN 1-57950-002-1 (alk. paper)
    1. Libraries and community--United States Case studies.
2. Library cooperation--United States Case studies. 3. Public
libraries-- United States--Administration Case studies. 4. Broward
County Library. 5. Libraries and community--Florida--Broward
County. 6. Library cooperation--Florida--Broward County. 7. Public
libraries--Florida--Broward County--Administration. I. Lynch, Sherry
II. Series.
Z716.4.L457 1999
021.2--dc21   99-14137
                                             CIP

Contents

> **Link** for *The Librarian's Guide to Partnerships*
> www.hpress.highsmith.com/lynap.htm

This book is gratefully dedicated to our partners who have raised our vision to a higher level, our performance to a higher standard, and our services beyond the box.

Forward: The Challenges and Benefits of Library Partnerships

The Librarian's Guide to Partnerships is intended to answer the question: "Why should librarians participate in community partnerships?" The thirteen chapters presented here were selected because they provide information on some of the partnerships that have significantly helped Broward County Library (BCL) meet the information needs of a broad range of citizens. They summarize the important lessons and benefits BCL staff, foundation members, friends, and partners have learned about the value of partnerships over the past twenty-five years. While every community differs in the type and number of potential public and private partnerships, we believe this handbook will provide some insight into the advantages of cooperation, and offer some practical solutions in removing barriers to these alliances.

The Challenges

Today, every library is facing important service delivery and funding challenges that necessitate forging innovative collaborations with community organizations and institutions. Addressing complex issues such as universal access to the Internet and declining literacy require all of us to proactively engage citizens, corporations, and community organizations in the life of the library. The process of building partnerships between diverse and often self-interested sectors of the community is a formidable challenge. Three important lessons that BCL has learned in overcoming our challenges are that time and patience are valuable allies and leadership commitment is crucial. We believe the lessons we have learned can be replicated by other libraries.

Taking the time, if possible, to get acquainted with potential partners by joining community organizations and participating in their activities establishes an important foundation for future collaborations. Often, potential partners don't know enough about each other's mission and need time to become familiar with the ways a relationship could be mutually beneficial. Potential partners who have gotten to know and trust one another are better able to maximize their commitments and rarely feel threatened by issues of "is it ours" or "theirs."

BCL staff have learned that being a tolerant, sometimes reticent, participant in community partnership discussions pays off in the end, and we'd recommend a similar sensitivity among any library staff that wishes to establish successful partnerships The likelihood of success increases when participants are able to check their egos at the door and focus on the service benefits to be achieved. Because the library is an institution intended to serve everyone, there isn't a particular agenda that has to be pursued. Therefore, issues can be given adequate time to develop and not be pushed to resolution before participants are comfortable and ready to reach agreement. Every worthwhile partnership has its moment in time and there is great value in being able to discern when to push ahead and when to wait for further developments. Good examples of this include a change in the political climate, the right funding mix, and space availability.

Every partnership encompasses one or more variables that will cause it to move ahead, stagnate, or fall apart. Among these variables, the critical one necessary to the success of any community partnership is the commitment of the leader(s) at the top of each potential partnership organization. An activist leader with a vision for what a partnership can achieve, the ability to effectively communicate and persuade staff to implement the goals of the partnership, is the all important variable.

As you will read, BCL has participated in many and varied partnerships to enhance and extend information services to our communities. These relationships have been necessary to the success of our service delivery system and we believe that librarians who seek affiliations and are active in their communities derive significant benefits for their efforts. These include:

- Deliberating with a partner and accepting the necessary trade-offs encourages organizational flexibility and risk taking.

- Engaging in community partnerships gives librarians valuable community leadership experience.

- Developing a wider span of community awareness through partnerships enables the library to more accurately plan for results and focus the mission and goals of the library on the information its community needs.

- Defining the library's mission in terms of community needs and interests shifts funding initiatives from outputs to outcomes—an important benefit at a time when governments and foundations are seeking community outcome data to support funding requests.

- Achieving the ability to more clearly identify how the community benefits from library services contributes to successful fundraising and more effective budget justification.

Results for the Community

Partnerships are invaluable because they introduce the library to people of all ages, religions, races, and economic circumstances. Many of these individuals have not previously used the library. Partnerships enhance basic services and enable the library to offer a greater range of specialized services. Partnerships extend scarce resources and bring us closer to meeting all the needs of the community. BCL's partnerships have fueled our growth and strengthened support for the library's mission of service.

SAMUEL F. MORRISON
Director, Broward County Library

Preface

Library partnerships—those participative, interconnected, entrepreneurial ways of providing information services—may be a new paradigm to many libraries, but at Broward County Library (BCL), the practice of partnerships has been standard operating procedure since before we were formed 25 years ago. The 35 branches, which today make up our system, are the offsprings of a grass-roots initiative to provide quality library service to a rapidly growing citizenry. These early citizen-based community collaborations created BCL by encouraging city-sponsored libraries to join a county-wide system and provided a working model for all the other partnerships that followed.

Twenty-two years after it all began in 1974, BCL was named *LJ*/Gale Research 1996 Library of the Year, in part, for our willingness to share resources and responsibilities with partners. Later that same year, we began working with Highsmith Press on the outline for *The Librarian's Guide to Partnerships* in order to share the "why" and "how" of BCL's partnerships and provide suggestions for others in the profession to use in developing their own partnerships.

The Librarian's Guide to Partnerships is intended to highlight a cross section of the more than 500 partnerships now in place and demonstrate through their activities how they brought new users and/or new resources to the library. The scope of the book covers the broad variety of partnerships that the library has participated in and documents the benefits, challenges, and developmental precesses common to each type. The chapters are laid out in chronological order beginning with Intergovernmental Partnerships and proceeding next with Education Partnerships, Other Libraries, Youth Service, Business, The Arts, and Specialized Partnerships focused on new Americans, diversity, and disabilities—for this is the way BCL's partnerships and our system developed. The chapters contain the stories behind BCL's affiliations and provide practical information for libraries just beginning the process of developing community partnerships. It should also be useful to experienced collaborators seeking new ideas.

Readers will learn how to be visible and active in their communities, how to approach pooling resources with private sector and nonprofit organizations, how to find common ground with other tax-supported institutions, and how to successfully leverage their existing affiliations to increase citizen use and support of the library, enhance library services, and develop staff leadership potential.

Envisioning, shaping, and actually completing *The Librarian's Guide to Partnerships* was a most challenging pleasure, not unlike the one felt by the myriad library supporters who visualized and brought forth our county-wide library system a quarter century ago. Many of those early advocates of quality library services are the human capital BCL continues to use to build effective partnerships. My greatest pleasure as editor is being able to acknowledge the efforts of these very special library supporters.

Citizen Partners—the supporters and advocates who recognize that a library is a vital community-based institution intended to serve everyone; those citizens whose efforts were and are responsible for positioning BCL as an essential community educational and cultural institution. BCL's important citizen partners include:

Broward County residents—the people of all ages, religions, races, and economic circumstances who request and receive our services and who, when satisfied with the outcome, have and will support our growth and development.

The Friends of Broward County Library—who were the essential catalysts in the grass roots development of our library system and who continue their vital advocacy efforts by keeping supporters and funders informed on how public funds are being used to improve the lives of county residents.

The Library Advisory Board, BCL's quasi-governmental liaisons to the Broward County Board of County Commissioners and library staff, who lobby for library funding and give voice to public discussions on important library issues such as intellectual freedom, access to the Internet, and building new libraries.

The 2,000 plus volunteers and docents—who give their time, talents and life experience to the library system—BCL's ambassadors who promote library service to non-users, new users, and the underserved.

Elected Municipal, County and State Partners—whose long-range vision and leadership have been demonstrated by a willingness to risk scarce public resources to expand and improve library services for all of Broward County's citizens.

The Broward Public Library Foundation—BCL's private-side partner, which has made significant contributions to library collections, services, programs, and buildings by developing funding relationships with numerous corporate, cultural, and individual contributors. Broward County's leaders who serve on the Foundation Board of Directors have been extremely effective in raising funds and public awareness for BCL.

Broward County Library Staff—who have accepted their important role in fostering and nurturing strong community ties as the key to positioning the library at the center of the community.

Gale Research and Library Journal—who selected BCL as their 1996 Library of the Year award winner primarily for the successful development of "countless strategic partnerships." BCL's staff and supporters are grateful for this wonderful honor and the very significant opportunities it has given us to heighten public awareness of the library and encourage even more fruitful partnerships.

I owe very special acknowledgments to my library and partnership colleagues who made the publication of *A Librarian's Guide to Partnership* possible:

To **Broward County Library Director** Samuel F. Morrison who accepted the invitation from Highsmith Press to share BCL's partnership experiences; who passed the editorship baton first to Shirley Amore and then to me; who guided, encouraged and complimented; and who, perhaps more than anyone else at BCL, recognizes that broad-based community interaction is fundamental to a healthy, thriving library.

To the **Contributing Editors**—Shirley Amore and Jerrie Bethel—each of whom gave crucial writing and editing support and were essential to the timely completion of the project. Shirley Amore, Sarasota County Libraries Director and BCL's former Associate Director for Central and Main Library Services, was the project's first editor and made important initial decisions about content and authors. Jerrie Bethel, former BCL children's librarian and now a librarian with the Freedom Forum in Arlington, Virginia, answered my pleas for help with copy editing. Her special insight helped me weave the singular stories each chapter told into an interconnected whole.

To the **authors**—Shirley Amore, Joann Block, Elizabeth Curry, Cindy Genovese-Shulman, Marlene Lee, Mary McBride, Jennifer Morrison, Samuel F. Morrison, Debbie Passalacqua, Tanya Simons-Oparah, and Jean Trebbi—who put aside their daily responsibilities at work and at home to tell their stories and share all that they have learned about growing partnerships.

Grass Roots Advocacy

by Sherry Lynch
Assistant Director
Community Relations & Partnership Development
Broward County Library

1

Background

Citizens living in Broward County in the 1960s felt they needed quality public libraries and recognized that an intergovernmental partnership between the county and its municipalities was the only way they were going to achieve their goal. Beginning in 1974, a group of citizen activists successfully encouraged five cities to give their libraries to our fledgling county-wide library system and over the next dozen years or so another nine followed suit.

The process of encouraging cities to join the system also encouraged citizen involvement in the life of their library and fostered valuable linkages between the library and the communities it serves. A successful bond issue campaign to construct new libraries in the late 1970s forged even stronger relationships that continue to the present time.

Building Together

As described further in chapters 2 through 4, partnerships with Broward County's education providers followed naturally after the development of the first intergovernmental affiliations for these institutions too were faced with rapid client growth and shrinking dollars. These partnerships include two joint-use libraries with Broward Community College, a joint-use partnership with Florida Atlantic University, as well as joint-use agreements with the School Board of Broward County. Each agreement has opened many new doors of opportunity and brought further involvement and support from other governmental bodies.

For example, when a second joint-use facility was being planned with the community college in Coconut Creek, city officials there were instrumental in lobbying both the county commission and the State of Florida for the necessary funding. This story has been repeated in the creation of several new branch libraries and of a joint-use middle school library just this year.

Further partnerships with civic and cultural organizations, corporations, businesses, individuals, and other libraries, benefiting both children and adults, also have developed and continue to flourish. Grouped together nongovernmental sources of revenue—foundation grants, individual and corporate donations, and others—play a significant role in creating higher quality, more in-depth specialized, or unique library service offerings and keep important private and corporate donors involved in library issues. Many of these are explained in the chapters that follow. It is also important to emphasize here that these supplements, no matter how generous, will never be more than a very small percentage of the annual revenue necessary to provide library programs and services to residents on an ongoing basis.

And so to the purpose of this chapter, which is to highlight some of the activities that keep critical governmental partnerships vital and growing.

Partnership Notes
Type: Government
Services: General library
Partners since: 1974

Wherever administrators and elected officials wish to improve public services and make more effective use of tax funds, they will find a way to develop and implement partnerships. The purpose of this book is to illustrate how one library was able to establish cooperative agreements with other entities, describe the problems and the successes that were experienced, and to share some creative alternatives that may be replicated by libraries in other communities.

Taking Care of Success

The shrinking of available tax-supported funding for libraries during the 1980s led to renewed focus on our intergovernmental partners: The Board of Broward County Commissioners, the 28 cities within Broward County, and the State of Florida. Members of the Library Advisory Board (LAB), Broward Public Library Foundation (BPLF) and Friends of Broward County Library undertook a program of library advocacy emphasizing the need to keep government funders and supporters informed about important library issues. A key ingredient in this plan was to take a closer look at the annual legislative breakfast.

Figure 1.1: Community Leaders, library supporters, elected officials, and partners attending the legislative breakfast at North Regional/Broward Community Library, November 1997.

Beginning with the system's twentieth anniversary celebration in 1993, the advisory board, the foundation and the Friends reformatted the annual breakfast for state legislators. It was reconfigured from a single event at the Main Library for state legislators into four regional breakfasts with an expanded invitation list that included county commissioners, city officials, business and community leaders, and library partners. This effort to bring funders and supporters together in a setting "closer to home" was very successful and achieved a number of important goals.

1. **Forum for officials to show support for popular library services.** It provided a forum where the focus of attention is the importance of library services. Each elected official attending is given an opportunity to talk briefly (one to two minutes) in front of his or her constituents about the library. This chance to address a large audience of citizens on a popular public service is the major inducement for officials to attend the breakfast. Over time a certain sense of competition has arisen among those officials attending and some wonderful testimonials have resulted:

    > *"library service in my community is like a contact sport..."*
    > **Mayor Norman Abramowitz,** City of Tamarac, Florida

    > *"... I'm proud to tell you that in my city we have more libraries (two) than McDonalds."*
    > **Mayor Ilene Lieberman,** City of Lauderhill, Florida[1]

2. **Forum for citizens to show support to officials for library services.** The breakfasts demonstrated to all the elected officials who attended that there was strong support for libraries. Two to three hundred citizens coming out at 7:30 in the morning to talk to legislators is significant. At one of the 1997 breakfasts, first-term state senator Skip Campbell, who had never attended a library legislative breakfast before, was so surprised by the number of people in the room that he shared his amazement and commented that he expected "ten or so people to show up." He went on to tell the audience how important it was for them to continue to advocate for libraries.

3. **The mix of citizens is also important because it provides a strong vision of a large "coming together" of people from many different perspectives and backgrounds with a common intent to promote libraries.** For example, library corporate partners and private donors have expressed important ideas to legislators about why they contribute resources to BCL. Michael Bienes, who has donated over a million dollars to the Broward Public Library Foundation, matched state funds for the construction of a rare book and special collections center at the Main Library. When he spoke at two breakfasts in 1995, he let our state legislators know that he was comfortable contributing to the library

because he knew the State of Florida had also made a financial contribution to the project. Demonstrating the effective use of shared public/private resources for important public projects like BCL's Bienes Center for the Literary Arts rare book department is a strong inducement to elected officials to continue support for library services.

At one recent breakfast a local African American poet actually composed a poem during the proceedings and asked to share her work with the audience. As a prelude to reading the poem "The Building of a Mountain," *(see page 4)* Mildred Keeve shared her positive experience of going outside her predominantly black neighborhood to seek library services at the Fort Lauderdale Branch Library. Her remarks and her poem moved everyone in the audience and demonstrated to all present the essential role the library has in the community.

4. **The legislative breakfasts bring our twenty-three local friends organizations together in a regional setting and successfully "model" what library advocacy is really all about.** Members of local Friends groups are sometimes hesitant to proactively advocate for library services. They may lack the confidence to make a personal contact with a legislator, preferring instead to leave these responsibilities to their board members. BCL's legislative breakfasts have been an opportunity for many of these Friends to gain confidence, meet Friends from neighboring groups, and to learn that the library advocates' real strength is their numbers. Just coming to breakfast, speaking with the folks seated on either side of them, and listening to what elected officials have to say is a very important growth experience in how to be an effective library advocate.

Friends who have been involved in arranging and hosting one of the regional legislative breakfasts are much more likely to proceed on to the next advocacy level—a visit with their legislators in Tallahassee and even the Congressional delegation in Washington, D.C.

Elected officials who have attended one library legislative breakfast invariably attend for a second time and then become regulars. The first name relationships that have developed between the board, the foundation and the Friends members and elected officials have smoothed the way for broader, more effective library advocacy in subsequent years. Over time, the library's support groups have become more skilled and therefore more comfortable and better able to keep our elected officials informed about the successful ways the library is effectively using public funds to change the lives of citizens.

BCL's strong program of advocacy paid off in fiscal year 1998 when the Broward County Board of Commissioners proposed a $39 million bond issue referendum for new, expanded, and remodeled libraries. So strong have relationships between the library's advocates and the elected officials become that, when asked for their support, both the Broward Legislative Delegation and the Broward League of Cities unanimously endorsed the bond issue.

This renewed momentum of library advocacy was, for the library, a key variable in the overwhelming 72 percent margin of victory in the March 1999 bond issue referendum. The enduring relationships between elected officials and library advocates plus the library's reputation as a system willing to share resources across governmental lines gave voters confidence that their tax dollars would be wisely spent. The bond issue revenue will build or expand even more partnership libraries. And in this way, the library's past, present and future will remain linked with its intergovernmental partners.

Notes
1. Mayors Abramowitz and Lieberman have since been elected to the Board of Broward County Commissions; both have remained strong library advocates.

The Building of a Mountain

A dream in the back of someone's mind
Lay dormant for years and years
The dream, so fragile just lay and hoped
That one day maybe reality would be theirs

No one believed the little dream
No one felt that it would ever be real
But the dream persisted, believed, and hoped
That somewhere, somehow they could see and feel

The dream was in Broward County Florida
And embodied one library for all
Children, grownups, handicapped
Of every color of the rainbow, short or tall

The dream chanced to meet some "grains of sand"
And the sand grains pledged their support
And united other grains to come and join
They did and brought more grains to the court

Little by little the mountain grew, rain only added strength
The rains and sand became one and stood tall
Then more and more until there stood a mountain
With strength, and power, and a hand for all

The dream of a library system
The people of Florida — the grains, you and I
Have bonded as one and now stand strong
No longer a dream, the grains are a mountain high!

Mildred Keeve
1997 Legislative Breakfast
North Regional/BCC Library
November 20, 1997

Broward Community College

by Debbie Passalacqua
Regional Supervisor
Broward County Library

2

Partnerships between public and community college libraries are still the exception rather than the rule. The following chapter summarizes the experience of two independent institutions in the successful construction and operation of two joint-use facilities.

Partnership Notes
Type: **Higher Education**
Services: **Joint facilities**
   & programs
Partners since: **1980**

A Handshake Between Friends

Some would say it was luck, or fate, or just plain old-fashioned good networking, but one day in 1980 a handshake sealed an agreement between two long-standing friends… and established a major precedent in library cooperation. Cecil Beach, who was then director of the Broward County Library (BCL), and Broward Community College (BCC) vice-president Dr. Clinton Hamilton each needed to build major libraries for their respective organizations. Beach's new regional library would serve a public library clientele in a rapidly growing area of southern Broward County. Hamilton's project was to build a new and expanded library for the youngest of Broward's four community college campuses, located in southwest Broward County.

Beach and Hamilton had worked together in various capacities throughout their careers, extending back to when Beach was state librarian of Florida. Hamilton, an ardent supporter of education, was also an effective library advocate and had recently been named president of the Friends of Broward County Library. With the climate of the times, each was anticipating an uphill battle to secure funding from their respective sources. Beach needed support from the Board of County Commissioners, and Hamilton required state PECO (Public Education Construction) funds. The two leaders were no strangers to creative management solutions, and they decided to try to pool their resources to create a whole greater than its two halves … the state's first combined public and community college library.

When it opened in 1983, South Regional/BCC Library was one of only a handful of public and community college libraries in the nation. Within a few years, it was considered by many librarians as a very successful program. Ten years later, when its sister library opened on BCC's North Campus, North Regional/BCC Library was only the second combined public and community college library in the state. Why has it taken so long for combined public and community college libraries to catch on, and what makes these projects in Broward County work so successfully? Read on!

Developing a Partnership Model

BCL's operational model in partnership libraries emphasizes service integration and contractual simplicity. The goal is for seamless interface of services; users do not need to wonder if they need assistance from a public library or academic library representative. As much as possible, all services are integrated. The simplicity of operation is grounded in a few key points basic to all Broward's joint-use contracts:

- Follow public library practices, except where exceptions are warranted.

- Local administrators are responsible for daily operations and determine which exceptions are necessary.
- Issues that cannot be resolved at the local level are referred up the chain of command for both institutions.

Clearly the success of this simple operational model depends on local administrators who, in managing the joint-use project, flesh out the services according to the spirit of the contract. (See page 79 for information about appendices on the Highsmith Press website, including the BCC agreement with Broward County.)

Bringing the Model to Life

Broward's higher education partnership libraries provide all the services you might expect in a quality public or academic library, but the four examples below serve as useful snapshots of operations:

Marketing

The public library and community college missions in outreach, programming and marketing are particularly complementary in a joint-use facility. The children who attended South Regional/BCC Library's story times fourteen years ago are today's college students. Is it any wonder some choose to return to the campus where they learned to be comfortable listening to Miss Marlene tell the story of the split dog? The library's role as a catalyst for lifelong learning spurs it to reach out continually to Broward's diverse community with programs, lectures, demonstrations and exhibits that present information in alternative formats. From the joint-use libraries come extraordinary community programs presented by college and university faculty members, dovetailing perfectly with college's motto that "Community is Our Middle Name." For the public library patron whose interest is engaged, even more wonders await at the library and in the college class of the instructor.

Collection Development

The contract for the BCC partnerships specifies that a specific dollar amount is set aside annually by BCL for materials selections by BCC. Public librarians work in concert with community college librarians to develop an integrated collection that serves the needs of both public and college library clientele. Because all the librarians serve all the patrons, it is in the librarians' best interests to develop a collection that truly meets the needs of all their patrons. When it is necessary to represent a special interest, both college and public librarians have varied subject expertises that can be depended upon.

Reference Service

Each joint-use library has a single reference service point at which public and college librarians work. Both college and public users are helped on a first-come, first-served basis by the next available librarian, regardless of whether that librarian is a BCL or BCC employee.

Bibliographic Instruction

Classes on library use are presented regularly to all incoming freshman English students. Both public and college librarians participate in the development of the curriculum and in the teaching of up to 60 library classes every semester.

Special Design Features in Joint Facilities

There is no better evidence of the integration of services at Broward's joint-use libraries than the design of their buildings. Imagine the delight of a college student and mother of a toddler who finds a colorful children's area in her "college" library.

Sharing the Work

Each of the cooperative facilities is jointly administered. Representation by both parties is critical to the success of each project. For example, although BCL operates the library on the North Campus of BCC under contract, a BCL regional librarian and a BCC North Campus director of library/ learning resources jointly administer services.

The division of labor breaks down naturally based on interests, abilities, and a few specifics in the contract for each library. Cross-participation in college library/learning resources committees, student and faculty meetings, staff development opportunities and other committee work constantly sensitizes the various players to each other's needs and provides valuable feedback.

Nearby is the popular materials area. Who would think that a college library would have the latest bestsellers, hot new videos, and the latest Pearl Jam CD? Something is different here!

The needs of each library's clientele dictate the design of the facility. Today's public libraries can be noisy and bustling places, so the joint-use libraries set aside a room for users who need quiet with minimal distractions. Tutoring rooms and group study rooms also benefit both public library users and college users. A Reserve Desk is the familiar academic solution to controlling access to required readings. Broward's joint-use libraries combine this function with their Periodicals Services. Staff at this service desk work with faculty and students to provide access to these materials exactly as would be done in a traditional academic setting.

Since the public library's audiovisual services complement college learning resources and lab services so well, it is natural to locate these services adjacent to one another. Remembering the goal of integrated service whenever possible, Broward's latest combined public and community college library actually has a joint Audiovisual and Learning Resources Service Desk. It is staffed by both public and college personnel cross-trained to serve the broad spectrum of user needs. Both clientele have access to the public and college audiovisual collections. The college audiovisual collection is for inhouse use only to assure that it is available for instructional purposes when needed.

Figure 2.1: The Youth Services room of North Regional/BCC Library. This fairytale seaport near the library entrance shows visitors children are welcome at this joint use public/college library.

Realities of Costs

It's a sign of our times that the star of joint-use libraries is on the rise. Resources are at a premium, and the concept of getting twice as much for half the price is a seductive one. Joint-use libraries have captured the imagination of library boards and college administrators across the country, due in part to Broward's successful ventures. Hardly a month goes by in the library without an inquiry from a joint-use investigative team. Of course, not every inquiry flowers into a successful joint-use venture. But a number of projects have recently been completed or are underway. Colorado's Front Range Community College at Fort Collins opened their joint-use library in early 1997, and both North Lake College in Irving, Texas, and Lake Sumter Community College in Leesburg, Florida, are currently planning joint facilities.

The process usually begins with a need: each partner needs improved access to library service in a cost-effective manner. By sharing resources, can the needs of each partner be met? Do the partners have—or can they develop—the trust in each other, the belief in each other's integrity, the vision and the common sense to compromise where appropriate to reach that vision together? The kind of relationship necessary to build a successful joint-use library doesn't happen overnight. The groundwork may even begin with a few shared endeavors not particularly associated with joint usage, as long as they result in a close relationship that leads to fruitful negotiations.

Broward County Library was certainly fortunate from the beginning with its higher education partnerships. The know-how and integrity of Cecil Beach and Dr. Clinton Hamilton were well known in the state, and after years of working together, BCL, BCC, and the Friends of Broward County Library had an advantage when it came to working out the details. Not every prospective joint-use partnership will be as blessed. But it must be emphasized that Broward's partnerships were the result of hard work, not luck. Years of cooperation before the first joint-use library was ever conceived paid off in these combined libraries in ways that no one ever dreamed of.

The single largest misconception about joint-use libraries is the idea that twice the library will result from half the cost, if each partner pays one-half. Broward's experience has shown it is more accurate to say *You get more library for more*. The pooling of resources allows each partner to get a bigger, better library than either could obtain individually. Because a joint facility requires compromise and accommodating the needs of both partners, the resulting library will have features and services that would not have been possible without the partnership. As a simple illustration, BCL's first regional library, which does not operate as a joint facility, is 40,000 square feet. South Regional/BCC Library, built two years later as a joint facility, has 64,000 square feet. Because of South's unparalleled success, North Regional/BCC Library was designed a decade later at over 100,000 square feet! More space, more features, more service, more staff ... cost more. But at the same time, each of the partners is underwriting only part of the cost, so the appeal of matching funds is almost irresistible to any funding body. Purchasing only one basic reference collection instead of two, one automation system instead of two ... the list is endless, and the funds a partner might have allocated for duplication of service can now be used to enhance service.

Facing the Challenges

Beyond the lure of matching funds, the urge to take advantage of other "freebies" is another siren's call. The potential for advances in programming, marketing, student recruitment, and service provision have already been discussed. Who can fail to be enthused about cutting duplicate spending and adding service enhancements? The missions of public libraries and community colleges are so closely related that it is probably the best-suited partnership of all the joint-use possibilities. But that does not mean that the partnerships are without challenges.

Classification Systems

Will the new facility use Library of Congress or Dewey Decimal Classification? The decision may be based, as in Broward's case, on which entity will handle materials processing in the future. Are there pre-existing collections, and will they be retrospectively converted? The costs of conversion are high, but maintaining two separate collections can defeat the purpose of a joint facility. On an even finer point, is one of the collections cuttered? The cost of re-processing is most likely prohibitive, but be aware of the long-term hidden cost of interfiling cuttered and non-cuttered materials. At Broward's joint facilities, shelving staff, librarians and patrons alike have had to learn how cuttered and non-cuttered materials are interfiled.

Automation Systems

The easiest scenario is when only one of the partners is automated, assuming that system can absorb the retrospective conversion needs of the partner. Far more complex is the situation where both partners are automated, and decisions must be made about which system to retain. Some multitype cooperatives have had to agree to work together to choose a new vendor. Whatever decision is made, the system chosen should meet the majority of prioritized needs for each partner. With the proliferation of area and state-wide networks, attention should be given to the ability to access information available through college and public library networks.

Organizational Values and Cultures

Each organization has its own structure, traditions, and operating style. Partners who intend to operate a joint facility must be willing to learn and respect what is important to each other, what is expected and valued by the members of each organization and how they operate on a daily basis. Are faculty members traditionally involved in major decisions that are made affecting library service? Do campus administrators expect to be notified in advance of major events at the library? As a major stakeholder on campus, does the public library administrative representative wish to be present at campus administrative meetings? Are members of each organization use to a collegial style, autonomy, or authoritarianism? Is one partner innovative or aggressive and the other more traditional or methodical? Are services client-centered or inwardly focused? True success of the venture depends on sensitivity to these holistic management issues.

The ultimate challenge in partnerships, of course, is the art of compromise. Broward's combined public and community college contracts have a few principles in common that guide the operation of the facilities: integrated collections; unified service points; open access to programs and services; major responsibility for most daily operations in the hands of public library staff; and major responsibility for facility maintenance, security and utilities belonging to the college partner. Details of how to dovetail the two institutions' policies into a working library are left to the administrators in charge of each facility.

The Development Process: It's All in the Attitude

After the historic handshake, all that had to be done was to work out the details. At BCL and BCC, earnest and devoted teams worked long hours hammering out the basics of Florida's first contract to jointly operate a public/community college library. There was no template to follow in developing the contract. Later, of course, this first contract would be used as a basis for developing future cooperative agreements.

When a leader has a vision, his or her staff can make or break the vision with their approach to the project. The secret to the success of the BCL–BCC partnerships is in the can-do attitude of the staff at each library. Not surprisingly, there is a direct relationship between the motivation of the staff to be successful, and the success of the partnership. Once the contract was signed, operations task forces comprised of representatives from both partnerships began meeting to establish common ground. A building design team gradually developed specifications for the state's first combined public and community college library. The ultimate architectural design by Oscar Vagi and Associates Architects, Inc. won the 1986 Governor's Award for Excellence in Public Buildings due to the innovative joint-use plan.

Shared facilities shouldn't mean shared confusion, so the partners in Broward decided up front to designate one partner as chiefly responsible for supervising the construction and the furniture/equipment orders. Change orders and fund accounting causes far fewer headaches with BCC acting as the agent rather than both organizations trying to divide up the responsibility. Each partner contributed one-half the cost of the new building, including furnishings and additional materials to flesh out the previously exclusively academic collection. Likewise, since BCL would be employing the majority of the new staff hired, they were responsible for hiring and training the 64 staff for the new library. These staff members would work side-by-side with college employees who report to different supervisors, work at different pay scales, have different schedule requirements, work under different work rules, and even have separate unions.

How to make it all work?

Attitude is the key. The whole story of Broward's successful joint-use libraries is summed up by a joint commitment to make them work, not to find reasons why they won't work. It is a heartfelt commitment to always make your partner look good, and never blame anything on the other organization. That same commitment is sought out in recruiting staff and encouraging existing staff through training and staff involvement. Local library administrators establish the right tone, plan and set goals accordingly, and staff follows through so desired objectives are achieved for both organizations. There are multiple channels for staff communication and user feedback, both formal and informal, so problems can be addressed when they are manageable and before they become crises. Operationally, each week brings another development, a compromise to be reached, or highlights two policies in potential conflict. Each week the partners invent a new way to make it work, together.

Attitude Adjustment

A story from BCL'S early joint-use days shows the importance of attitude in a successful partnership library. At a faculty meeting, Dr. Hugh Adams, who was then BCC President, listened gravely to the concerns expressed by his staff, weighing the evidence they presented about why the partnership wouldn't work. Dr. Adams thanked them for expressing their concerns and said two simple sentences: "Ladies and gentlemen, this project **will** work. Now, it will either work with the people sitting around this table..." Pausing, he made eye contact with each person around the table, "Or it will work with other people." For a moment all breath was suspended. Then the participants began to say, "You know, we think this project is going to work!"

Learning from Broward's Experience

After sixteen years of operating libraries in cooperation with higher education institutions, what has Broward learned?

Joint-use libraries deliver more for more, not more for less

Building design and operation is more expensive than for a building half its size that either partner might build separately. More staff is necessary due to added services and to serving a broader clientele than either partner would serve alone. A more generous materials budget is needed to meet the needs of a larger customer base. But the synthesis of public and community college resources creates a library that is truly greater than the sum of its parts.

The importance of representation cannot be overestimated

Partnerships are not very successful if decisions are made unilaterally. Through experimenting with various operational models, Broward has settled on co-administration in its joint-use facilities. A BCC Director of Library/Learning Resources and a BCL Regional Librarian with equal authority work out the operational details for each library. The benefit is that each side feels their interests are represented on a daily basis. Ensuring that each partner has representation lessens the urge for territoriality and reduces feelings of being threatened.

Location, location, location

If a combined public and community college library is located on a college campus, then placement on campus is crucial for marketing the library to the public. Of course, location of the campus itself determines the degree of usage by the public as well. Broward County Library's joint-use facilities are in heavily populated areas on the edge of campus. They are placed as close as possible to a major thoroughfare, rather than in the center of campus as would be traditional for an academic library. Parking requires special consideration for joint-use libraries, too. Ample convenient parking must be provided for the public. Knowledge of the student population and the community surrounding the library is used to estimate peak usage hours for college students and public library patrons. Whether college and public usage hours complement each other or coincide must be taken into account in planning parking.

Maximize the partnership advantages while meeting challenges directly

Joint-use libraries are a golden opportunity to earn the respect and support of users who appreciate the prudent use of their tax dollars. At the onset, potential users sense they have essentially twice as much library for only half the cost—what a great deal! Now give them *value* for their money. Take advantage of special partnership opportunities such as jointly sponsored programs and co-developed grants. The North Regional/BCC Library building program incorporated a new day care center for the children of faculty and students as well as members of the public. The joint funding enabled both partners to reach a long-awaited goal, securing convenient day care for their employees' children. Joint operation will also fine-tune both partners' problem-solving skills. Be ready to devote special attention to collection development and weeding, academic freedom versus employee harassment, and Internet access policies.

Higher education's secret recruiting tool is partnership libraries

The promise of South Regional/BCC Library's opening fourteen years ago is today a reality: graduates of the library's story time are becoming Broward Community College graduates. Why? Because they perceive Broward Community College—

through its library—as a friendly, caring place. Because they are comfortable there. Because it has a remarkable library with an especially service-oriented staff. But yesterday's children are not the only ones attracted to BCC by its library. Working people and senior citizens, job-seekers and displaced homemakers, people with disabilities and a variety of people from all ethnic backgrounds benefit from library programs, have a chance to interact with college personnel through the library, and decide that they, too, can improve their lives by taking a college class or two.

Joint-use libraries are better libraries

Joint-use collections are stronger due to the in-depth knowledge of college faculty who participate in the materials selection and weeding processes. Community members definitely benefit from circulating access to college-level materials that might otherwise not be available to them. Joint-use library staffing is stronger because they are required to have teaching skills and subject expertise to work successfully with college faculty and students. Community relations are enhanced for both organizations through partnership libraries. For example, Broward promotes the college in its public library outreach efforts, while the college promotes its libraries as one of its primary strengths. The college's campus security is another significant benefit for Broward's joint-use libraries. Well-trained security guards are an asset in any emergency, and contribute to a positive atmosphere of safety for users of all ages.

Exceed Your Wildest Dreams with a Partnership

Little did BCL and BCC know where a simple handshake would take them! Broward's combined public and community college libraries today are widely recognized as model joint-use facilities, and both organizations enjoy popular support because of their innovative and creative partnerships. The libraries are among the most heavily used in the state, with usage growing daily.

The Future

After sixteen years of joint usage, what does the future hold for Broward? The South Regional/BCC Library is located in the most rapidly growing quadrant of Broward County, and is heavily used beyond optimal levels. Experience with the new North Regional/BCC Library, 40 percent larger than South Regional, further highlights the need to expand Broward's first joint-use library. When plans are complete, the expansion and renovation will, of course, be a partnership project.

With technology developing at lightning speed and user sophistication escalating apace, the future also brings challenges for joint-use libraries in service design and delivery. Collection development is shifting from traditional print resources to electronic information sources and non-print resources. An increasing percentage of the budget must be spent on computer software to address college needs for computer-assisted instruction. These needs must be balanced with the still-increasing demand by public library users

Figure 2.2: The Learning Resources Lab at North Regional/BCC Library provides computer assisted instruction, word processing facilities, and tutoring services for college students as well as instructional materials and academic support services for faculty.

for more popular materials. Currently under development is a virtual reality bibliographic instruction module that may soon replace some in-person instruction by librarians, or at least substitute when a student happens to miss the class at the library. The future probably holds some additional challenges when it comes to reconciling public library and college policies on full graphical Internet access. That's nothing new for Broward. They'll find a way to make it work, somehow.

Florida Atlantic University

by Mary McBride, Ph.D.
Vice President for Broward Campuses
Florida Atlantic University

3

Defining the Need

Partnership Notes
Type: Education / Post
  Secondary
Services: Joint facilities
  & programs
Partners since: 1984

Florida Atlantic University (FAU), headquartered in Boca Raton, is one of the ten universities which constitute the State University System of Florida. The Florida Board of Regents has assigned FAU a service area which extends over one hundred miles on the Atlantic seacoast from the Broward County–Miami/Dade County border through Palm Beach County north to St. Lucie. In the early 1980s, FAU was struggling to define its mission in this rapidly growing region of South Florida and especially in Broward County, where the board of regents also assigned some responsibility for higher education to Florida International University (FIU), whose headquarters was in Miami/Dade County. Broward County, with more than one million residents but without a state university of its own, was thus sandwiched between Palm Beach and Miami/Dade Counties, where the two state-supported South Florida Universities had their respective main campuses. As Robert Dressler, a former Fort Lauderdale mayor and board of regents member, described the situation in 1987, "Historically, Broward County has been getting the short end of the stick in higher education."

The increasingly powerful Broward legislative delegation was determined that its citizens should have the cultural and economic benefits of a university located conveniently within the county. The city of Fort Lauderdale, the seat of Broward County government, saw a strong university presence as a fundamental necessity for growth and economic development. The Fort Lauderdale Downtown Development Authority helped to create a civic vision of a revitalized downtown filled with government agencies, a large library, a performing arts center, a university and community college presence, a museum of art, and other cultural and governmental organizations complementing a dynamic private sector. The Fort Lauderdale Chamber of Commerce was also an aggressive supporter of this vision of an arts and sciences district in the midst of a governmental and financial center. Martin J. Kurtz, Chairman of the Downtown Council, said that "to be competitive, Broward County must have its fair share of Florida's higher education dollars as well as some 'catch up' funding."

The Board of Regents appointed FAU to take the lead in the construction of a University Tower in downtown Fort Lauderdale, and funds were appropriated for a ten-story building to be constructed adjacent to Broward Community College's (BCC) downtown offices. The facility was to provide space for BCC and FIU as well as FAU. This project benefited from the serendipity of the county's plan to build the Main Library just one block from the site of the planned University Tower. It made good economic sense for the university and the library to form a partnership which would enable BCL to function also as the academic library for the University Tower. City, county, state, and university officials endorsed the plan. On a visit to Fort Lauderdale, in 1984, then Governor Bob Graham toured BCL, saw the construction site of the new university building and affirmed the idea of combining local and state resources for a multi-functional library facility which would serve both public and academic needs.

13

Joint Facility a Reality

A public library also functioning as an academic library? Despite the skepticism of some faculty members and library staff, FAU, on behalf of the board of regents, prepared an agreement with Broward County which defined the terms and conditions under which the downtown public library would enter into a partnership with the university. (See page 81 for copy of FAU/Broward County Agreement.) In 1985, even as construction was proceeding on the University Tower, the Florida legislature appropriated funds to be employed by BCL to purchase the library resources necessary for the university programs planned for the FAU downtown campus. The appropriation included funds for both library materials and personnel services, although the allocation was spent primarily on books and serials selected by the university faculty and librarians. These materials were also included in the total university library materials inventories.

During the first two years of the partnership, funding was at a higher level to support the new programs, provide services, and supply the materials to build BCL's collection to the level demanded by the university programs, which included graduate degrees in public administration, urban and regional planning, and business administration. Since the inception of the partnership, funding has remained fairly constant, although the recession of the early 1990s negatively impacted state funding, as did the necessity to transfer some funds to the university's new and rapidly growing campus in the suburbs.

Funding for People and Services

Library funds were divided into four general categories, including personnel, equipment, supplies, and library materials. Three librarians were employed and assigned to the technical services, circulation, and reference departments. The partnership impacted almost every area of BCL's operations: acquisitions, receiving, cataloging, processing, circulation services, reserve activities, reference services, bibliographic instruction, online services, administration, financial accounting, and reporting. Since this was prior to public access to computers, typewriters and other equipment were purchased, and in 1989, when the computer-based Southeast Florida Library Information Network (SEFLIN) was constituted, a small portion of the allocation was used to support university membership.

FAU was the fiscal agent for the legislatively appropriated funds used to provide the services specified in the partnership agreement, and, after each legislative session, transferred the appropriation to be used to support the masters and doctoral programs to the Broward County Main Library. The agreement itself contained all the provisions required by the respective government agencies and clearly spelled out the terms and conditions governing the use of the appropriation. It specified that university librarians would initiate specific requests for library materials or would specify subject areas for approval of purchases by public librarians. BCL retained the right not to accept any university library materials for custody and/or circulation which its governing authority might reject. In that unlikely event, those items would be returned to the university.

The agreement provided that although BCL would process and handle the materials according to its current procedures, the books and other materials were the property of the university and would be so indicated on or in each physical unit. The general public, as well as university students, staff, and faculty, would have access to the materials. It was agreed that the Main Library would attempt to recover any loss or damage incurred by patrons to items in the inventory in accordance with the policies and procedures applied to materials in the public collections. The partnership agreement also provided that BCL would maintain the same general library services and hours of operation for the university students, staff, and faculty as it provided for its regular clientele. BCL would provide to FAU an OCLC/MARC-compatible tape record of its holdings for inclusion in its university database. Interlibrary loan service was especially important to the university community in need of material for research. The first point of access for interlibrary loans was SEFLIN.

All members of the university community would be treated as Broward County residents with access to the books, equipment, and services provided by BCL. But certain exceptions were stipulated. For example, semester-long borrowing privileges were granted to university faculty teaching in Broward County as well as to graduate students. In addition to FAU, which the board of regents named the lead university, FIU, the University of South Florida (USF), and the University of Florida (UF) also taught graduate courses in Broward County. Provisions for reserve book operations, bibliographic orientations for individuals and for classes, reference assistance, and use of audiovisual media were all included in the agreement.

Although there were only a few university/public library partnerships across the nation at this time, Dr. William Miller, Director of FAU Libraries, stated that "this innovative arrangement is a win-win situation for everyone: the public has full access to research-level materials not normally found in public libraries, and the university has access to facilities and services without having had to build or provide them." Miller also noted that "the public is a clear winner in this situation because the university has funded the purchase of hundreds of thousands of dollars worth of books and journals each year, material which is freely available to all, and which has greatly enhanced the purchasing power and the materials collections in the Broward County Main Library." However, Dr. Miller acknowledged that faculty members and students have special needs that differ greatly from the library needs of the general public.

Facing the Challenge of Accreditation

From the beginning of the partnership, BCL's staff was flexible in its policies, receptive to change, and determined to do all that was necessary to make the partnership work. At first, however, some faculty members remained skeptical and considered the library services, indeed the downtown campus generally, something of a backwater (they were allowed mileage expense for the trip to the Boca Raton campus library). Much of the credit for changing these attitudes and making the necessary partnership accommodations on the university side goes to Dr. David Prosperi, then chair of the Department of Urban and Regional Planning. Dr. Prosperi also chaired the University Tower Library Committee and worked tirelessly over a three to four year period to craft the policies and procedures which made the library an attractive and useful resource for university research.

Dr. Prosperi believed that most of the faculty concerns were directed more toward the issue of service than the collection itself. For example, the Library Committee helped to make everyone concerned more sensitive to the university's need for policies that allowed circulation of materials for a longer period than that allowed the public. Maria Treadwell, FAU Broward Coordinator of Library Services, supported Dr. Prosperi's viewpoint. Preparing for the first-ever accreditation of the Master of Urban and Regional Planning, Dr. Prosperi, as chair of the Department of Urban and Regional Planning, commissioned a study in 1991 by Elizabeth Bryne of the University of California, Berkeley, which revealed that the services at the library needed major improvements. Eileen Cobb, then director of the Main Library, took immediate pro-active steps to provide the necessary training and policy changes that would result in improved services. Connor Tjarks, Assistant Director of FAU Library Administration, and Ms. Treadwell also actively sought out faculty concerns and assisted in making improvements.

Because the University Tower is the headquarters of major academic programs in architecture, urban planning, public administration, and the Graduate School of Business, the size, diversity, and currency of the collection must meet the standards of several regional and national accrediting agencies as an important criterion of the accreditation of these academic programs. According to Dr. Dennis Gale, current Chair of the Department of Urban and Regional Planning, the Planning Accreditation Board approved the department's Master of Urban and Regional Planning degree accreditation in November 1994, subject to the completion of a Progress Report on additional library acquisitions. This requirement, however, was a product of the department's youth, not a result of the library's public status. A plan to enlarge the collection was implemented. On November 15, 1996, the Planning Accreditation Board accepted the department's Progress Report as submitted. "In the intervening four years," Dr. Gale reported, "we have continued our quest to build solid holdings in planning monographs and serials." Dr. Gale praised Ms. Treadwell's resolute efforts to assist the department in her role as university liaison to the Library staff.

Dr. Charles Washington, Director of the School of Public Administration, helped to bring the school through its national accreditation review. He noted that the "traditional range of library service, from reference to reserve, to audiovisual, to general circulation, plus the technology-oriented services, such as online access, searches, databases, and inter-connectivity with the state library system, video cassettes, and the special reference assistance, combine to offer an excellent resource to primarily graduate public administration students."

The newest addition to the academic community of the downtown campus is the School of Architecture. Dr. Peter Magyar, Founding Director and Professor, is now in the process of preparing for the national accreditation of the School of Architecture, whose standards emphasize the adequacy and quality of library resources. He believes that the library is an indispensable tool in the education of an architect. The library staff is assisting the faculty in the selection and acquisition of new books, slides, tapes, compact discs, serials, and other materials. The physical location of the growing collection has been rearranged, and plans have been made to place architectural journals close to the new home of the school in a university building now being designed.

As an important financial center in South Florida, Fort Lauderdale is an attractive and strategic location for the university's Graduate School of Business. The FAU College of Business won high praise and unconditional ten-year reaccreditation for all its programs at the conclusion of the rigorous examination process required by the American Assembly of Collegiate Schools of Business in 1998. Among the nation's thousands of business programs, only 115 carry the distinction of being fully accredited through the doctoral level. Masters and doctoral business programs at FAU are headquartered at the University Tower. According to FAU Broward Associate Dean Ken Wiant a Peer Review Team Report assessed FAU's unique service area and concluded that a distributed campus model was needed to service that area. Dr. Wiant reported that the accreditation team "specifically reviewed the quality implications of the model with respect to the three primary campuses (Boca Raton, Davie, and Fort Lauderdale) served by the college and found that all the elements that would be expected in a single campus environment were present in the distributed model." Dr. Wiant is pleased that with respect to library resources available for the college as a whole, the AACSB team found that they are excellent, with a special mention of the available access to electronic data sources.

Benefits for the Community As a Whole

Other aspects of collaboration between the university and BCL in downtown Fort Lauderdale include partnerships of direct service to the community. In 1995, a Public Policy Lecture Series was cosponsored by the library and the School of Public Administration and brought speakers such as Dr. Eugenie Price, Senator George Mitchell, NASA Astronaut Dr. Bernard Harris, Jr., and James Burke, author/public television host of the science series *Connections* to the library's downtown auditorium. The School of Architecture presented lecture series in 1996 and 1997 in cooperation with the library, bringing a diverse group of internationally known architecture experts to Fort Lauderdale. The university benefits from the programs which the library sponsors through the Florida Center for the Book and the Bienes Center for the Literary Arts. The FAU College of Liberal Arts, which is headquartered in western Broward County, will be a partner with the library in the creation of a research program at the soon-to-be-built African-American Research Library and Cultural Center, long a vision of Library Director Samuel F. Morrison. University-sponsored poetry readings, art exhibits, and musical performances are given space in the library auditorium on a frequent basis. Faculty and staff enjoy the unique relationship and seek creative ways to extend and enhance it for the benefit of the urban community. For example, an analysis of the electronic resources of the downtown cultural and arts organizations has recently been inaugurated, with an eye toward greater inter-connectivity of those resources. And the library will serve as a resource for a planned Urban Laboratory School, a full-service school partnership among the public schools, BCC and FAU.

Figure 3.1: Invitation to the Urban Architecture lecture series.

In this as in any partnership endeavor, problems still arise. For example, a faculty member complained that a staff member at first refused to allow him to keep a novel in his possession longer than the normal circulation period because it was not really "academic," despite the faculty member's protest that it was required reading in his management class. The solution? Better staff training. Students want even longer hours of operation and more available serials and databases. The solution? Another look at budgetary priorities. Flexibility of response to these "customer" complaints by the library staff, the Library/University Advisory Committee, and the university administration is essential to the smooth working of this model. From time to time, BCL staff is invited to attend Faculty Senate meetings, and invitations to university cultural and social events are regularly extended. In a complex partnership, cooperation cannot thrive without frequent communication on several organizational and human levels.

Since the university/library partnership was ultimately created to accommodate and to benefit students, it is appropriate that they have the last word in this description of its origin and operation. And what a positive last word that is! According to MBA student Omer Ipekci, Chairman of the FAU Broward Student Government Graduate Council, students think that the partnership should be publicized more widely in the community because residents of Broward County will "feel good" as tax payers knowing that the partnership is "a smart way to stretch resources." It is gratifying that students recognize that this partnership is indeed a cost effective means which improves the quality of life of citizens even as it provides a needed university resource.

Note: Material for this article was contributed by Dr. William Miller, Dr. Dennis Gale, Dr. David Prosperi, Dr. Charles Washington, Dr. Ken Wiant, Dr. Peter Magyar, Maria Treadwell, Connor Tjarks, Eileen Cobb, Sherry Lynch, Kevin Janser, and Omer Ipekci. I take full responsibility for any errors of fact or interpretation. Hearty thanks to all the contributors.

School Board of Broward County

by Cynthia Genovese-Shulman
FDLRS Media Center Coordinator
Broward County Library

4

Partnership Notes
Type: Education/ Primary-
  Secondary
Services: Joint facilities,
  programs & collections
Partner since: 1992

School children and teachers are traditionally among the biggest consumers of public library collections and services. However, there are relatively few examples of cooperative agreements between schools and public libraries designed to enhance this relationship. The public often assumes that these partnerships exist, but in fact, most are simply informal relationships with uncertain lines of communication.

The two projects described in this chapter; the Florida Diagnostic Learning Resource System (FDLRS) Media Center and the Professional Collection, are both examples of how a school board's need for improved access to educational resources and a public library's goal of providing better service to its users can result in an effective partnership that benefits thousands of people. Because similar needs and opportunities are likely to exist in many communities, it is hoped that ideas for new partnerships will grow from these successful projects.

Background

The Broward County Public School District is the fifth largest and one of the fastest growing districts in the nation. In the 1995–1996 school year, 191 elementary, middle, high, adult/vocational, and center schools served approximately 208,000 K–12 students and 240,000 adult students. The School Board of Broward County is one of the largest employers in the county, employing 20,266 full- and part-time employees, including 11,125 teachers. As the population has grown, so has the need for space, services and facilities. Within the past decade, more than 70,000 new students have enrolled in Broward County Public Schools. In that time period, 57 new schools were built and 150 underwent renovation. Critical overcrowding remains a problem with many new schools bursting at the seams. Over the past five years, the school district has focused on streamlining administration to redirect funds to the classroom.

School Board of Broward County Professional Collection

The life of a teacher is a little bit easier in Broward County because of a collaborative partnership between the school board and the library. In addition to the demanding responsibility of serving a rapidly growing and diverse population, teachers are required to take in-service classes and additional course work to maintain their state teaching certificates. Many teachers are working on advanced degrees at local universities. After teaching all day, thousands of teachers in Broward County are going on to classes at night, on weekends and throughout the summer. Much of their free time is spent on reports, practicums, projects and theses.

Today, thanks to the efforts of the school board and the cooperation of Broward County Library (BCL), any Broward County teacher can call the professional collection liaison at the Main Library with a request for specific titles or journal article citations that are needed for their coursework or classroom curriculum. Books are retrieved, articles are copied, and materials are sent via the school board's delivery system to their school, saving them much time and energy.

School board administrators, school board members, special committees, and task force members are also able to call the professional collection liaison with requests for special searches and specific information. Information has been provided for the superintendent's office in areas such as busing, charter schools, cultural diversity, and standardized test scores, model standards and content specific standards. The up-to-date information helps the board make informed decisions.

By relocating its collection and services to BCL's Main Library, the school board has exponentially increased the amount of information and materials available to its staff. In addition to its own collection, the entire BCL library collection is available to educators.This is supplemented by the education materials of Florida Atlantic University and Florida International University, along with all other county library services, including the online and CD-ROM databases, plus the interlibrary loan service.

History

Before its move to the Main Library, the School Board's Professional Collection was housed at the Learning Resources Department in a school board building in the southwest corner of the county. It was available only during regular school hours. The collection contained materials related to educational practices and research, curriculum design and development, and a retrospective history of education. The service provided had been highly specialized, and Learning Resources staff provided assistance to educators with their research. The holdings were accessed through a book catalog.

The incredible growth of the student population in Broward County resulted in a great demand for more schools. In the early 1990s, the superintendent began informal discussions with the library director to explore the idea of relocating its library of professional materials to the Broward County Main Library. The Main Library was already serving as a joint-use facility for the general public, academic institutions, and other contracting agencies. It seemed appropriate for schools to enter into this collaborative partnership.

Process

Once the decision was made to transfer the Professional Collection materials to the public library, it was time to address the nuts and bolts details. A contract was drawn up for approval by both governing bodies. As discussions between the Learning Resources staff and library staff evolved, both sides realized they would have to compromise to insure the success of the partnership.

The school board's collection included 66 standing orders and 54 journal titles. The first issue to be resolved was whether periodicals should circulate. The school board's policy allowed for circulating periodicals. Broward County Library's policy did not. Library and school board staff looked at the real issue—how to ensure that teachers could get the articles they needed. It was decided that articles could be copied at the library and sent through the delivery system to teachers and school board administrators. Rules regarding use and the total number of pages followed library regulations, copyright laws and fair use guidelines. These guidelines had to be communicated to teachers.

Merging the journals collections coincided with large increases in periodical costs. The merger allowed for consolidation and some very welcome savings for both parties. The money saved allowed both parties to actually purchase additional journals and materials during a time of cutbacks for many libraries. Without increasing its serials budget, Learning Resources was able to test new journals in subject areas such as technology in education, Internet and schools, attention deficit disorder, literacy and education for students at risk.

The Learning Resources Department also had an ERIC collection dating back to 1969. The Government Documents collection at the Main Library had an ERIC collection which was started in 1980, when the facility opened. By merging the two collections, the library was able to provide a contiguous ERIC documents collection.

Because shelf space at the Main Library is finite, and in keeping with BCL's Collection Development Policy, the school board was also asked to weed its collection. Multiple copies were removed from the collection, taking its size down from 9,000 copies to 5,483. The library's collection development team was brought in to identify any remaining duplicate copies. Duplicates were offered to the regional libraries.

However, since the School Board felt strongly about the importance of a retrospective as well as a current collection in order to support research into the history of education and curriculum, BCL had to make exceptions to its collection development and weeding policies, allowing older books to remain in the collection.

Cataloging and Conversion

The next phase of the integration was to process and catalog the materials. School Board staff at the Learning Resources Department completed the physical processing which included stamping "Broward County Library" on the top of the book," MN/SBBC" on the book pocket, inserting security tags, and placing the library logo on the front cover.

The Professional Collection's shelf list was sent to OCLC and an electronic record was created. BCL cataloging staff provided original cataloging when there was no matching record. The collection went from a book catalog to MARC record. The materials were linked in the database with a special note indicating ownership by the School Board. A shelf list can be produced whenever needed and circulation statistics for the collection are generated monthly.

There were many advantages to having the collection online, including improved access for teachers with dial-in capabilities from home or school. Teachers would no longer have to search through a list of several thousand titles to find the items they need. By checking the library database they could also determine whether a book was available or currently checked out. New items added to the collection showed up immediately, whereas a book catalog was out of date within days of being printed. Once this conversion was completed, materials were shelved according to their Dewey number in the Main Library.

The transfer of the Professional Collection materials was begun in August of 1992 and completed in March, 1993. The School Board financed the moving of materials, shelving, furniture and equipment into the Main Library according to the contract. It also paid for conversion of the catalog to MARC record and provided additional funds for the purchase of new materials and subscriptions.

Services

The next step was to focus on defining the scope of services to be provided. As mentioned earlier, the teachers and School Board staff had been accustomed to a high level of personal service from Learning Resources staff. SBBC staff wanted to ensure that teachers and administrators would continue to have this type of assistance. The contract included the employment of one part-time library assistant to operate the professional library and $10,000 to maintain and expand the collection. The library assistant would provide reference materials and assistance in their use as well as information and referral. This staff person would also be responsible for preparing orders and maintaining materials and budget information.

As a result of the contract, the following services were provided to teachers: loan of books and audio-visual materials; copying and sending or faxing of journal articles; telephone reference service; interlibrary loan and SEFLIN (regional cooperative library) services; delivery service to and from the Main Library through the School Board's delivery system to local public schools; online searches for School Board administrators; ERIC fiche retrieval and reproduction; and cataloging and processing of new materials.

By contracting out this service, the School Board Learning Resources staff was freed to focus on training, outreach, literacy, technology, automation, and helping establish new media centers. BCL took over supervision of staff and service, along with acquisition, processing, cataloging, shelving and circulation. In the four years since the collection moved to the Main Library, over 12,000 materials have been circulated. The continuing addition of online databases and access through SEFLIN Freenet has allowed teachers much greater access to information. The collection is now available seven days per week, including evening hours, and it is accessible online twenty-four hours a day.

Challenges and Evolution

As with any change, there were some needs which had not originally been anticipated. Since all of the staff at Learning Resources had provided library service, it was difficult to determine the amount of time that would be needed for the Professional Liaison at the Main Library. A library assistant position was originally funded at twenty hours per week. The first two years of operation saw frequent staff turnover resulting in disruption of service and placement of orders. Staff were using the position as an entrance into the county library system and then left after their probationary period was complete and a full-time position became available.

The liaison was trained in many different operational aspects of a public library; ordering, maintaining a budget, interlibrary loan procedures, circulation functions, use and reproduction of microfiche, serials and copyright procedures, as well as how to search various online databases. The expectations of the School Board were for a high level of service which included research, personal reference assistance, and a quick response time. It became apparent that in order to achieve these goals the position needed to be upgraded to professional status and made full time.

When the FDLRS staff relocated to the 4th floor of the Main Library in December, 1995, the newly hired Professional Collection Liaison joined them in their offices and began to assist at the FDLRS reference desk. This not only facilitated the training of the new liaison, but it also allowed for smoother flow of services for teachers. They could contact one central point, the FDLRS Media Center desk, and have their educational questions addressed seven days a week, either by telephone or walk-in. They were also able to take requests for periodicals or materials and forward them to the liaison.

With the 1996-1997 contract, the position was reclassified to a full-time Library Specialist I. The Professional Collection Liaison now has time not only to provide reference assistance, but to concentrate on collection development, planning for delivery of services and program management. The Liaison has been able to work with other library staff to set up a computer program for processing book orders and has been able to generate bibliographies for teachers. The next step is to increase marketing of this service to teachers.

Summary

The merging of collections has resulted in an improved public library collection. School Board funds are being used to support trends and key issues in educational theory and practice. The partnership demonstrates that two large bureaucracies can work together to improve service to their public.

Those libraries considering merging the local school district's professional collection into their public library collection should consider the following:

1. Your target population is educators. Be prepared for detailed reference questions.

2. The liaison should be prepared to perform all aspects of library work- from performing detailed research on educational issues to verifying citations, copying articles, and retrieving and circulating books.

3. The liaison needs to be linked to a department where he/she can get ongoing training and have a supervisor available to provide direction and feedback.

4. Be prepared to have other staff continue to provide the service contracted for during any staff vacancy.

5. Be willing to compromise on your weeding procedures.

6. Be prepared to deal with the rules and policies of two different systems.

7. Remember to give yourself extra time for the contract to be approved.

8. Have a plan for continuing staff salaries if an adjustment is delayed by the bureaucratic process beyond the beginning of the new contract year.

9. Negotiate contracts that provide for an increase in the salary and materials budget.

10. Enjoy the satisfaction of helping teachers improve the education their students are receiving.

Florida Diagnostic Learning Resource System Media Center

Introduction

The phone rings in the Florida Diagnostic Learning Resource System (FDLRS) Media Center on a Saturday morning. One of the FDLRS Media Center staff picks it up with a friendly greeting. On the other end is a woman in tears.

"Can you help me?" she said. "I was at a meeting at my son's school yesterday and they told me he was mentally retarded. What does that mean? Will he be able to get a job, get married, have a family, live in his own place?"

On another day, a family walks into the FDLRS Media Center and approaches the reference desk. "Can you help us?" the mother says. Our son's pediatrician thinks our son might be autistic. We need to learn what that means."

On a Sunday afternoon a teacher of emotionally handicapped and learning disabled students comes into the media center and says, "Help! I've been transferred to a new school and the teacher before me took everything that had been in the classroom. I'm desperate for reading and math materials."

On another day, a university student approaches the FDLRS reference desk and says, "I have to give a 60 minute presentation on autism and I know nothing about it. Do you have any videos or books that will tell me all about it and how to treat it?"

These are the types of queries raised at the FDLRS Media Center, a special library for parents, teachers, community agency representatives and university students living, working with, or studying exceptional students.

The wide variety of exceptionalities served include: autism, down syndrome, educable mentally handicapped, emotionally handicapped, gifted, hearing impaired, multiple-handicapped, physically impaired, profoundly mentally handicapped, specific learning disabled, trainable mentally handicapped, and visually impaired.

What Is FDLRS?

The collection housed in the Broward County Main Library includes over 7,000 items in a variety of media types: kits, books, videos, games, manipulatives, cassettes, and serials. The materials in the collection provide information on exceptionalities, inclusion, special education law, as well as techniques for managing behavior, enhancing self-concept, and developing self-help and social skills. A variety of curriculum programs and approaches are available to patrons.

The typical day includes as much telephone reference as walk-in assistance. Most of the regular and special education teachers access the media center by phone during the school day. Requests for materials can be phoned in or sent through the Broward County School Board's delivery system, which makes regular stops at the Broward County Main Library.

On the weekends, teachers and university students spend time using special kits and other materials, networking with one another, researching and planning presentations, and sharing ideas. Families come in looking for materials that will help them deal with behavior, improve reading and math skills, help their child with readiness skills and communication or otherwise enhance their child's development.

The children coming to the Media Center might be in wheel chairs or using a communication device. They might exhibit unusual behavior, have verbal outbursts, or stand unmoving in one spot. They might also have invisible disabilities such as specific learning disabilities or traumatic brain injury which result in many different types of learning and behavioral challenges. All of them are welcome.

Every parent coming to the FDLRS Media Center also has the additional benefit of access to the Family Network on Disabilities (FND), a support and advocacy group for parents of exceptional children. Located within the FDLRS Media Center, the FND office is staffed by parent volunteers who have practical experience raising children with disabilities. They are experienced in dealing with schools and are aware of various programs throughout the school district for exceptional children.

The parents working in the Family Network on Disabilities Office are able to provide parents with information on their child's rights for an appropriate education. They are able to explain to parents the types of accommodations the Americans with Disabilities Act (ADA) and the Individuals with Disabilities Education Act entitles them to request for their child.

The Family Network on Disabilities can also connect parents with other parents of children with the same type of disability, as well as with local, state, and national support groups. They co-sponsor sibling workshops designed to help children of disabled brothers or sisters deal with their feelings. Several of these parents are responsible for monitoring local discussion groups on the Internet. Their presence in the Main Library provides a unique resource for people concerned about improving the quality of their exceptional child's life.

Historical Background

The FDLRS Media Center is part of a continuum of services provided by FDLRS (Florida Diagnostic and Learning Resources System). FDLRS is a statewide program that provides services to special education students, their teachers, and their parents. There are nineteen FDLRS centers in the state of Florida. Each FDLRS center provides diagnostic and instructional support services to Florida's exceptional student education programs, with media services being one component under the Human Resource function.

FDLRS services include a referral system called Child Find for persons ages 0-21 who may be exceptional but are not receiving special education and related services. Staff at the FDLRS Media Center are able to refer parents and grandparents to Child Find when they have a concern about their child's development. Patrons coming to the library not only have access to information and materials relating to child growth and development and exceptionalities, but they can also be referred to an expert who can determine whether or not a child needs further screening.

Thanks to this service, many preschoolers have been evaluated and placed in preschool exceptional student education programs. Having information available and providing referrals for this type of service greatly benefits families in the community. In 1996, access to this type of information was expanded when youth services librarians throughout the system were made aware of this service and Child Find flyers were made available at all 35 branch libraries.

FDLRS also provides information to educators, parents, and community members through public awareness activities, involvement with community agencies, and distribution of publications which highlight upcoming events. Broward County School District publishes a quarterly publication, *The Parent Calendar,* which is sent to all parents of children receiving exceptional student education services in Broward County. This calendar is available at the FDLRS Media Center and at all branch libraries. Through this calendar, university students, parents and grandparents are all able to contact local support groups and exceptional student education district staff for help and information.

FDLRS also develops and delivers in-service training based on district priorities, current trends and issues of interest to teachers, parents, and support staff in every area of exceptional student education. In order to support in-service training and district priorities, the FDLRS Media Center collection of books, kits, curriculum materials and videotapes are available for loan through the Broward County Library. The FDLRS center in Broward County was the first in the state to locate its materials in a public library.

Media Center History

The FDLRS Media Centers were developed in the 1970s in order to support the efforts of Florida schools to comply with Public Law 94-142, otherwise known as the Education and Mainstreaming Act. This act stipulated that children be educated in the least restrictive environment. Teachers needed help in finding materials that would be effective with exceptional students who did not respond well to traditional or standard curriculum.

The State Bureau of Student Services and Exceptional Education allocated funds to add a media component to FDLRS services. For close to fourteen years the media component in Broward County was housed in a School Board complex which was open on school days and during regular school hours. Teachers and community agency representatives coming in were required to register and document that they were providing educational services to an exceptional student in order to have access and borrow materials.

By 1991 plans were underway to move district staff into the new district office building in downtown Ft. Lauderdale. The FLDRS coordinator was informed that due to limited space the media component would need to be located elsewhere.

The FDLRS coordinator began her search for a new home for the collection of over 14,000 items. She needed a facility that was large enough to house the collection, was more centrally located than the media center's former location in the Pompano Beach Multipurpose Center, and offered the means to properly display, circulate, and protect the materials. She saw several benefits in relocating the center to the Main Library for the people who needed the FDLRS collection:

1. Increased hours, including weekends;

2. Access to the Talking Book Library, which is located in the same building;

3. Proximity to the Kathleen C. Wright School Administration Building;

4. Access to additional related materials including the School Board's Professional Collection, already housed at the Main Library and, collections from Florida

International University (FIU) and Florida Atlantic University (FAU), which are also housed in the Main Library.

The Broward County Library Director saw the benefit of having additional materials and a specialized collection which would increase the library's service to teachers, parents of exceptional students and university students.

A place was designated as a "Parent Corner" where parents would be able to peruse newsletters, brochures, and materials to obtain a quick overview of the latest services and programs for exceptional students on the local, state, and national level. Little did the library realize how important this service, including the office of the Family Network on Disabilities would be to parents of children of all ages in the community.

Process

Initially, two library staff visited the media center, which was located in an old high school that had been converted to a multipurpose center. A good bit of the collection was mildewed or had parts and pieces missing. The library staff felt the collection needed a major overhaul before moving it to the Main Library.

The relocation to the Main Library also required a workable computer system complete with circulation, registration, patron data, overdue notices, media maintenance, cataloging, searching and report functions. FDLRS had been using three different computers to perform all of the required functions. Both agencies agreed there was a need for a computer system that would handle all of the media center's needs. FDLRS agreed to hire a consultant to design a system that would provide the required type of library records and functions and generate required grant statistics.

The FDLRS Media Center was closed for the 1991-1992 school year to allow for this reorganization and weeding of the collection. During this time, all materials were barcoded and entered into the new computer database.

Contract Negotiations

While this was being done, the School Board and county attorneys were negotiating the details of a contract for media services between the School Board of Broward County and Broward County Government. Under the terms of the contract, the library agreed to operate the FDLRS Media Center as a separate department within the Main Library. The Libraries Division agreed to comply with all requirements of the state grant that applied to the FDLRS Media Center and its collection of materials. (See page 85 for a copy of the master agreement between the school board and Broward County.)

The contract provided funds for the hiring of one Librarian II, one Library Associate, and three Library Assistants. The staff hired were employees of the Broward County Library, and functioned under the library's job descriptions, job titles, and pay scales. One person was transferred from the School Board of Broward County to Broward County as a Library Assistant.

The contract provided for the transfer of money to the Libraries Division for staff only. The library agreed to provide space to house and circulate the FDLRS collection, space with electrical outlets for storing and displaying adaptive/assistive materials for evaluating students, as well as electrical outlets for the operation of several computers. The contract also insured that space would be allocated for a preview area to accommodate filmstrip, audiocassette, and videotape previewing. It stipulated that the periodicals would be commingled with the Main Library's collection.

Opening

In June of 1992, FDLRS moved its 13,000 item collection into a highly visible glass enclosed room of approximately 5,000 square feet on the first floor of the Main

Library. The new center also included an area with Apple computers intended to be used for teacher workshops, previewing of educational software, and student assessments. This area grew and developed into an assistive devices demonstration area which later became part of the Broward Community Technology Center in 1996, another collaborative partnership between the Broward County School Board and BCL.

In August of 1992, the FDLRS Media Center opened its doors to serve the people working with exceptional children in Broward County. The next year was an incredible learning experience for the staff of both Broward County Library and the Broward County School Board.

Juggling Two Bureaucracies

Once the doors opened, a new phase began. The first year required on-going training and meetings between the two agencies. Through patience, communication, and clarification on both ends, day to day concerns and operational details were sorted out. Staff used to county procedures and the features of a large system had to adjust to another bureaucracy with its own language, acronyms, and way of doing things.

The School Board agreed to install signage and provide all office equipment, supplies, and telephones. Any materials needed for day-to-day operation of the media center had to be requested through the school district.

Any printed materials distributed at the FDLRS Media Center had to be approved by the administrations of the School Board and the Library prior to distribution. Printed pieces such as brochures and flyers had to go through the channels of both bureaucracies. One of the early lessons learned was to allow extra time for any project.

Refining Computer Operations

FDLRS Media Center staff were trained on a customized stand-alone computer designed for the department by a consultant who had never programmed a library computer system. The first several months involved many meetings with the programmer to refine sections of the database and correct programming errors as they became noticeable. A reservation system was installed. The database was not arranged in MARC format and staff soon learned the machine was not very forgiving. A misplaced hyphen or the deletion or addition of an article or word could negate the search. The system did not allow for combined or Boolean searching. A good bit of the data entry work had to be corrected over time as errors were noticed. Key words and new terms had to be added to facilitate searching.

One of the unique features of the system which five years later still gets rave reviews from patrons is the bibliographic function built into the database. Specialized annotated bibliographies can be produced by exceptionality, subject, grade levels, key word, or media type. Thousands of bibliographies have been given out to FDLRS patrons. Teachers can fax, phone, or send in their requests to the FDLRS Media Center after looking at their bibliographies, and their materials can be sent to their school through the School Board's delivery system, which makes a stop at the Main Library. Parents of handicapped children can take these resources home and look at them at their convenience.

Another unique feature of the computer system were the required state grant reports. These computer generated reports were able to provide a breakdown by specific type of patron; exceptional student education (ESE) teacher or specialist, regular education teacher, community agency representative, parent, university personnel or student, or volunteer, as well as the number of items each personnel type checked out.

Identifying the FDLRS Patron

Another issue that challenged the library staff was the correct identification of a
FDLRS patron. The FDLRS Media Center staff were given specific criteria to use to
interview a potential patron to determine if they met the grant eligibility guidelines.

The School Board provided the media center with nearly a foot high stack of
computer printouts listing School Board staff and all students classified as ESE. In
order to register to be a media center patron and check materials out, a teacher's
name had to be listed on the computer printout as a special education teacher. The
regular classroom teacher was asked to provide the name of a student in her class who
was receiving exceptional education services. Staff had to find the child's name on
the printout as well.

Parents of exceptional children 0-21 had to present proof of their child's exceptionality if their child's name was not on the computer printout. They were required
to bring in the child's IEP (individual education plan), or a psychological evaluation
outlining an exceptionality.

University students were required to bring a letter from their professor stating
they were taking a class related to exceptional education which stipulated that the
professor agreed to be responsible for the materials and withhold grades if they were
not returned.

The library staff, who were accustomed to doing everything possible to meet the
information needs of all their patrons, now had to tell some people they were not eligible to borrow materials. Certain conditions such as attention deficit disorder and
tourette's syndrome were not considered exceptionalities. If a child was over 21,
their parent or service provider was not eligible to check out materials. Although
anyone was welcome to come in and use the materials in the media center, these
parameters remained a cause of concern for the media center staff. It became a goal
of the media center librarian to ease the eligibility criteria for registration and
improve access for more of the community.

Location and Visibility Redefine Clientele

Another very interesting development that took place the first year of its operation
was the increased use of materials by parents and representatives of community agencies. Because of its visibility and accessibility, many people walked into the media center to find out what it was. Many of these people knew or lived with someone with
exceptionalities. Librarians throughout the system began referring parents and
grandparents to the FDLRS Media Center for information. Midway through the first
year of operation, the School Board FDLRS liaison confessed that previously he
could have counted on one hand the number of parents who used media center services. By the end of the fourth year of operation in the Main Library, nearly 800 parents with exceptional children had registered with and used the FDLRS Media
Center.

Representatives from various community agencies also came into the FDLRS
Media Center and asked about accessing materials. While the School Board had provided a list of five community agencies they considered eligible to check out materials, the media center coordinator, working with library patrons coming in to the center, identified close to thirty five additional community agencies that were providing services to exceptional children. By putting the media center into a public library
building, the School Board took a giant step towards moving services for handicapped children into the mainstream. Within two years after opening its doors at the
Main Library, material use had quadrupled and a whole new group of people were
FDLRS patrons! This occurred at the same time as the movement towards greater
inclusion of children with disabilities in their neighborhood schools and communities was taking place throughout the nation.

State Funding Cut Results in Reorganization

After two and one half years of operation in the Main Library, FDLRS funding for the media center was cut at the state level. The nineteen different districts in Florida were told funding for the media center components of their budgets would no longer be forthcoming. FDLRS coordinators were told to think about giving the media component of their programs away. In Broward County, the FDLRS coordinator fought tenaciously to preserve a program that had received many kudos and was cited as a prototype for the rest of the state.

The FDLRS coordinator began meeting with the Main Library Director and FDLRS Media Center Coordinator to explore how they could continue to provide service to parents and teachers of exceptional children. She was able to commit funding from the other components of her budget to support three positions. One of these positions would be assigned to the new technology center when it opened. Library staff looked at how the cut from five to three staff would impact provision of services. It was determined that if FDLRS staff could be relieved of cataloging and circulation functions; i.e., patron registration, circulation, generating and sending overdues, they could devote more of their time to patron reference needs.

Figure 4.1: The Assistive Technology Educational Network Regional Lab.

It was decided to convert the FDLRS collection to MARC records to add them to the BCL database. Not only would this allow Broward County circulation staff to take over those circulation functions, it would also make the collection accessible on all library public access computers, as well as to patrons with dial-up access from their computers at home. Because the collection was being converted to BCL's database, the School Board also agreed that anyone with a library card who felt they needed access to the collection would be entitled to use it. The goal of the media center coordinator to increase patron access was going to be realized!

The decrease in the number of funded positions also required a rethinking of how to make the best use of the remaining staff in the department. The center was located in a self-contained room on the first floor that required at least two people in the room in order to serve FDLRS patrons, answer directional questions, and aid regular library patrons using the assistive technology housed in the room. The remaining staff would not be able to staff the room on the first floor. At the same time that FDLRS media services were being re-organized, the Libraries Division and the School Board of Broward County were exploring the possibility of opening a jointly operated technology/computer center. It made perfect sense to relocate the media center to another floor in the building and use the enclosed room on the first floor for the technology center. By relocating, the staff would be freed from over 1,000 directional questions every month and would be able to focus on the needs of its FDLRS patrons.

Figure 4.2: Patrons selecting assistive devices in the FDLRS Media Center.

The hours of operation were changed to Monday-Saturday, 9-5, and Sunday, 12-5:30. With the relocation to a floor with other staff and services, it would be possible to have one person at the reference desk most of the time. Other library staff would be on the floor to ensure adequate security. Materials would be available all hours the library was open.

The move up to the fourth floor necessitated other changes as well. Since the conversion was going to be outsourced to OCLC and the space on the fourth floor was more limited, another major weeding was done to prepare the collection's database for downloading and shipment to OCLC. The seven hundred educational, speech, developmental and psychological tests which circulated from the media center were relocated to Nova Southeastern University, where they could be accessed by psychologists, teachers and university students who were performing assessments and doing screenings of students. This part of the collection was never intended by the School Board to be used by the general public. Over 1,000 pieces of computer software were removed from the database and transferred to the FDLRS instructional technologist, who assigns them to particular ESE students or teachers. The database was reduced to approximately 7,000 items.

Reorganization Results

In December of 1995, the FDLRS Media Center moved to the fourth floor of the Main Library, the same floor which houses the education, medical, social services, and child growth and development materials. As the FDLRS books were converted they were integrated into the regular collection, joining the materials owned by FAU, FIU, SBBC Professional Collection, and BCL. This pooling of materials strengthens the collection and enhances what Broward County is able to offer the community. This integration of materials has also resulted in improved, computerized management of overdue materials. At the same time that the move took place, the new Professional Collection Liaison began reporting to the FDLRS Media Center Coordinator. This reorganization enhanced library services to educators by giving them one location to visit in the library for assistance in locating educational materials and planning their research.

Library service to other types of patrons has also been enhanced. Occupational therapists, home health nurses, physical therapists, literacy and church volunteers are using FDLRS materials with clients or family members with various physical or medical problems. Parents of children with attention deficit disorder now have access to the materials. Parents who want to learn more about their child's learning style or who want to help with homework use FDLRS materials. Parents of homeschoolers are discovering and taking advantage of the collection. Circulation of materials is increasing even with the reduction of the collection through weeding.

Future Challenges

Planning FDLRS library service for the future includes the need for a collection development plan that will allow the quality of the collection to be maintained as its use increases. Additional funding will be needed to keep the collection current and replace materials as they are worn. Management of the collection needs to allow for continued weeding as well as adding to the collection over time. Because the collection had been purchased with grant dollars, the School Board was initially very hesitant to weed. In its former locations, when the collection grew, the School Board added more shelving or moved to another School Board building. This is no longer feasible.

The next challenge is to see how use and needs evolve with the expansion of the patron database. New and different types of materials might be needed for the new patrons taking advantage of the service. Examples of new types of patrons include a former English literature professor who used FDLRS reading kits to work on her comprehension and reading skills after suffering a traumatic brain injury which put her back at a 3rd grade reading level and a mother who adopted two homeless children who had been living in a car. She used the reading kits available at FDLRS to work with her children and discovered they were not mentally handicapped as originally diagnosed.

Future goals include a survey of patrons to determine their needs for materials and services. Always important will be the need for flexibility, adaptability and anticipation of change. Through vision, leadership, and commitment, a very important service was maintained and made much more accessible. With continued support this program should continue to offer valuable resources needed by the many individuals who are living or working with an exceptional child.

Summary

Providing this type of service in a public library benefits the library, school board and parents. The library receives the benefit of adding to its holdings and increasing its patron base. The school board benefits from the expertise of professional librarians, extended hours, technology and a much greater pool of information. Parents benefit by having access to current information and by gaining assistance in obtaining information and materials that will help them care for their exceptional child. Parents often find a public library more accessible than a school.

Librarians considering a collaborative partnership of this type need to consider the following:

1. Have a clear focus and mission.
2. Be prepared for negotiation.
3. Expect the contract phase to be tedious.
4. Be prepared to deal with the rules and policies of two different systems.
5. Know your target population.
6. Be willing to compromise.
7. Expect and plan for delays.
8. Anticipate and expect change.
9. Be ready to learn.
10. Select a department head who has a basic knowledge of child development, educational practices and terminology.
11. Select a staff that is flexible.
12. Lastly, be prepared for an exhilarating and touching journey.

Conclusion

In the past several years projects have flourished by combining the resources of the School Board of Broward County with BCL. The Library System recognizes it is in the information business. It remains responsive to institutions as well as individuals that approach it with a need. By focusing on cooperation and opportunity, it will continue to flourish.

SEFLIN and SEFLIN's FreeNet

by Elizabeth Curry
Executive Director
SEFLIN

Background

In 1984, a group of librarians in South Florida came together with a vision of cooperation and a quest for the best service for library users. This vision resulted in SEFLIN, the Southeast Florida Library Information Network, which is committed to the facilitation of resource sharing, cooperative use of technology, and innovative partnerships. The Broward County Library (BCL) was one of the founding members of SEFLIN, and it has continued to actively support the organization's projects.

SEFLIN was the second multitype cooperative library system (MLC) established in Florida. It was established with federal grant funds as a demonstration project under the leadership of Florida State Librarian Barratt Wilkins. The funding source was the federal Library Services and Construction Act (LSCA), and Kathleen Imhoff, BCL assistant director, wrote the original grant proposals. BCL administered the funds on behalf of the SEFLIN members, and provided office space for the fledgling organization. The arrangement was so successful that SEFLIN continues to lease office space and the computer room from BCL at a substantially reduced cost. Today SEFLIN is known regionally and nationally as a leader in collaboration and innovation.

The grant money was an incentive, but the heart of multitype cooperation is based on a strong philosophy and commitment to quality service. Furthermore, SEFLIN members had a strong belief that they could achieve more by working together, than by working alone. They had a wide array of resources, a willingness to share them, and a commitment to apply their collective expertise to help one another. SEFLIN's mission and values statements reflect this spirit, and they can be found at the end of this chapter.

Structure

SEFLIN is governed by a board of directors, who are generally directors of the member libraries. There is also a representative of the associate member libraries, who is a non-voting member of the board. The library directors actively support and guide the organization and they appoint people from their staffs to serve on SEFLIN committees. There are fourteen standing committees which address areas such as reference services, cataloging, serials union list, government documents, collection development, interlibrary loan, library management, and technology. Over 150 people serve on committees, and their contributions are significant. Our Strategic Plan provides direction, but the committees are responsible for implementation. They develop the action plans and submit annual reports to the board. The committee leaders have established five roles for committee members:

1. Develop regional rapport and cooperation. Committees provide a forum for librarians and library staff to develop rapport and share information and expertise.

2. Give advice to SEFLIN staff and board. Committees provide the means for representatives of SEFLIN members to give SEFLIN staff feedback and advice.

Partnership Notes
Type: Multi-Library
Services: Joint collections, training, programs
Partners since: 1984

Figure 5.1: SEFLIN logo.

3. Innovate and increase productivity. Committee members actively participate in joint projects to experiment with innovative products, to enhance services to users and improve resource sharing.

4. Promote continuing education and training. Committees identify needs and plan events to improve staff expertise.

5. Coordinate and communicate within the member library. Committee representatives provide information concerning SEFLIN projects to others in their libraries and seek input from them.

SEFLIN staff act as committee liaisons. There are ten SEFLIN staff positions plus a variety of part-time contractors. Their role is to support the member libraries, to guide, coordinate, plan, facilitate and evaluate joint projects. SEFLIN staff also provide leadership to the members. This leadership is generally of a collaborative nature. It is based on listening, watching trends, understanding library needs and proposing solutions. It is based on empowering groups to become partners.

Projects

A combination of access and delivery services have been the mainstay of the SEFLIN services While the technology has changed since 1984, when SEFLIN was established, two of the original SEFLIN services still operate today: the fax network and the daily courier delivery service. Both of these services were developed in order to share materials among libraries and to better serve library users. The courier began as a partnership using BCL and Miami/Dade County Library vans and drivers. The arrangement was so efficient and effective that it still operates through a SEFLIN contract with these libraries. Early in SEFLIN's history telefacsimile was the newest high technology tool. SEFLIN libraries created a telefax network to quickly send articles from one library to another. Using a federal grant, fax machines were purchased for all SEFLIN libraries. The most important aspect of the project was the development of interlibrary loan standards and policies which all libraries could agree to follow. This tradition of cooperation was also the foundation of the document delivery project in 1993 using ARIEL software. BCL and Miami/Dade Public Library were two of the first public libraries in Florida to incorporate ARIEL software into the interlibrary loan procedure.

One of SEFLIN's most important products is a serials union list which is maintained on OCLC. The SEFLIN Serials Committee established standards for the list and it continues to monitor quality control. SEFLIN has produced this list for member libraries in paper format, microfiche, and CD-ROM. The CD-ROM is available as either a stand-alone product or through the SEFLIN CD-ROM Network. This product is widely used by library users and staff. The impact of the SEFLIN Serials Union List, courier, fax network and other SEFLIN bibliographic products can be seen in the very high interlibrary loan rate, the very high fill rate within the region, and the high number of articles (versus monographs) requested.

Training

SEFLIN's members constantly use the system to experiment with new services. Essential to this effort is our continuing education and training program. We have established a continuous learning environment called the SEFLIN Academy to meet the needs of members. SEFLIN staff conduct training sessions, drawing upon the expertise of staff from libraries in the region. We hire contract trainers, frequently from SOLINET. Committee members are actively involved in deciding the training schedule and the topics. Some committees also conduct peer training during their meetings. Many of our cooperative projects involving technology emerge through the identification of new technological products and trends. One way that SEFLIN

There are several factors which have been critical to SEFLIN's success:

- The directors and staff of SEFLIN libraries care about quality service.

- SEFLIN has been truly "member driven." The participation and initiative of every member has been critical.

- Staff of SEFLIN libraries know each other and communicate frequently.

- Members are committed to maintaining local resources and seeking cost effective ways to enhance services in a cooperative environment.

- Libraries commit local funds to collaboration and pay SEFLIN membership dues that range from $5,000 to $35,000.

- Decision making is done by consensus, not just majority. People think of how the whole group can succeed, rather than just how their library can benefit.

- SEFLIN members are continually looking at trends for the future and ways to become partners.

- SEFLIN members are innovators who seek ways to surmount obstacles.

- SEFLIN members break down barriers in their quest for improvements. SEFLIN members don't ask "Can this be done?" Instead they ask "How can we make this happen?"

- SEFLIN libraries acknowledge success and celebrate together.

assists members is by sponsoring vendor showcases to demonstrate and evaluate these products

Continuing education takes many, many different forms. SEFLIN sponsored our first uplink teleconference, "Who Will Govern the Web?" which was accessed by 44 sites in fourteen states. Originally, the program was to be held at Palm Beach Community College and feature national speakers. In order to extend access to the event, SEFLIN sponsored the uplink with special financial contributions from BCL, Palm Beach County Library System, and Palm Beach Community College Library. Biennially SEFLIN's Reference Committee organizes a conference called "Energizing Information Services." The purpose of this program is to offer a keynote speaker and breakout sessions for librarians who may not be able to routinely attend conferences outside the region. In May of 1998, SEFLIN hosted the ACURIL Conference (Association of Caribbean, University, Research and Institution Libraries) for 280 librarians from 27 countries. SEFLIN libraries provided volunteers to staff many activities during the five day conference. BCL actively supported ACURIL and hosted a reception sponsored by SIRS Inc. which featured plans for Broward's Afro American Center.

Another special project developed in 1997–98 is the SEFLIN SunSeekers Leadership Institute. This institute provides six sessions throughout the year to candidates nominated by library directors. A mentoring program is also part of the leadership development. Broward County was instrumental in developing the project and enrolled four people in the first year. In commenting on the impact, Kathleen Imhoff, BCL's assistant director, noted "There was no real opportunity in the region for our staff to obtain a high level of external library leadership training. We needed this type of training for our system, so I worked with SEFLIN's Library Administration and Management Committee to make it happen."

The type and format of continuing education and training programs vary but the overall purpose is to bring new information and inspiration to the region. Organizing the workshops, special events, showcases and institutes is a cooperative process. There is a partnership between the SEFLIN staff and committee representatives as needs are identified, topics are researched, formats are developed, presenters located and events are scheduled.

As a precursor to the Z39.50 standard, SEFLIN pioneered the use of IRVING software to provide a common command structure to linked catalogs in the late 1980s. In the early 1990s, SEFLIN offered joint subscriptions to CD-ROM databases mounted on a CD-ROM network. This was part of building the "library without walls." Today, SEFLIN libraries are exploring ways to create a virtual library catalog, to allow users to search multiple catalogs with one search, and to offer new options for interlibrary loan. Distance learning technologies are challenging us all to look at different ways to share resources and serve users. The library without walls concept is still valued as we look to new technologies to help us offer better services to library users.

SEFLIN Community Networking — Free-Net

During the SEFLIN strategic planning process in 1992–93, the member libraries stated their desire to enhance the libraries' role in providing local, government and community information to Southeast Florida residents. As SEFLIN board president, Samuel F. Morrison proposed the development of the SEFLIN Free-Net, a community-based information service. Rather than developing the project just in Broward County, Morrison proposed the development of a regional service which would have greater impact. BCL pledged $10,000, use of the library's dial access lines, and a staff person (Shirley Amore) to assist SEFLIN staff in developing a pilot project.

The technical staff of both SEFLIN and BCL coordinated the project, which touched staff at every level of the library. BCL provided the dial access lines and

SEFLIN provided a server so users could go directly to either Free-Net or the BCL WiseGuide. As a pioneering partner in the Free-Net, BCL began by training staff to use the online service and to assist users with Free-Net. BCL staff made hundreds of presentations to community groups and put posters and displays in each library to register people for accounts. An Electronic Groundbreaking Ceremony and Electronic Ribbon Cutting Ceremony were held to announce the beginning of the project.

It is significant that the advisory committee formed for the pilot project consisted of representatives from throughout the region. Everyone had the opportunity to participate in policy making—not just those in Broward County. While the project started in BCL, its purpose was to test a system that would serve the entire region. BCL launched it as a regional project, for its administration and staff had the vision to recognize it offered greater benefits to their constituents. Control was never an issue because it was a collaborative project. The SEFLIN Free-Net opened in Broward in 1994. It was soon swamped by the high use.

The project expanded to Palm Beach County and Miami-Dade County with toll-free access and content in 1995. Martin County became a partner with toll-free access and content in 1997. SEFLIN libraries have been pioneers and this project has been recognized as a model of cooperation. The access, the local content, the training classes and cooperative efforts have made this project an overwhelming success. The SEFLIN Free-Net was the second free-net or community information network (CIN) in Florida. It is the only CIN in Florida managed by a multitype library cooperative. It is believed to be the first free-net in the country developed and operated by a multitype library cooperative. It is important to remember that the SEFLIN Free-Net is serving four counties with a population of over four million people, one-third of the population of Florida. The partnership allows each county to maximize the impact of their funding and resources. Without a cooperative approach, the resources of each county would be stretched thin.

The web is a technology. The Free-Net is a philosophy. The Free-Net is more broadly directed and partnership oriented. The web is a collection of information. However, the popularity of the web definitely has affected the use, content and development of Free-Net. Community networking began when the technology was only one step removed from bulletin boards. The web has brought the Internet to more prominence. And it brought more people online than ever before. But community networking is still more than just being online. A Free-Net or Community Information Network is built "by the community, for the community." Many different community groups, information providers and volunteers are involved. Libraries have a tradition of community outreach, local information, and access which all fit into community networking. A key part of a Free-Net is that it allows community groups to load and maintain local information on the Internet, using a web server. It empowers groups that may not have access to a server. Another essential library philosophy which relates to Free-Net is free access to information. There are several types of user populations: 1) groups that use Free-Net to load local information, 2) local users who access the Free-Net/information from home or office via the web, 3) local users who access the information via free dial access lines, 4) local users who go to the library to use computers and access Free-Net, and 5) global users who access local South Florida information from other cities, states, and countries via the web.

The SEFLIN Free-Net is truly a community resource. Libraries provide the leadership, and staff of member libraries devote many hours promoting the service, training community groups to load local information, training users to find information and organizing information online. SEFLIN libraries use Free-Net to empower groups to create and maintain their own web pages. To make the project a success SEFLIN established a variety of committees. These included a Free-Net Training Committee (library staff – regional), Free-Net Local Content Committee (library

Free-Nets

Free-Nets are a brand or type of community networking (CIN).

Free-Nets are **not** just websites with local information and links.

Free-Nets are **not** just public access to a free Internet connection.

Free-Nets are **not** just free e-mail.

The community networking movement is based on working closely with community groups to get information online, to promote communication within the community.

Community networking is done "with" the community, not just "for" it.

staff – regional), and Free-Net Advisory Committees for Broward, Dade, Palm Beach and Martin Counties (each composed of community members). In addition some communities have contributed through the creation of Reference, Government Documents, and Technical Committees.

The SEFLIN Free-Net Training Committee and Local Content Committee are examples of partnering and collaboration on many different levels. The committee members work together to develop tools to use for training. They share their ideas and expertise. The committee members assume responsibility for representing Free-Net to the users and potential users. They train additional staff from their institutions to assist in a variety of roles. The committee members also provide feedback on policies and planning. There is a general misconception that everyone is on the web, knows how to use the web and has access to the web. The use of the web is growing dramatically each day, but there are still a very large number of people who need access and assistance. SEFLIN staff and committee members have created a network of trainers who offer free classes in libraries. Since 1994 there have been an average of 800–1,000 people a month trained by staff of member libraries.

SEFLIN staff members have worked with library staff since 1994 to develop programs for local information providers. SEFLIN library staff members working with Free-Net have found that people from local organizations generally do not know how to organize, prepare or technically load information on the web. People are interested but somewhat apprehensive. Many groups lack equipment as well as technical expertise. SEFLIN libraries offer space on the Free-Net server for community groups that do not have the budget for commercial services, as well as training and ongoing support.

As of February of 1998, there were 223 individual information providers from 189 organizations with over 6,000 pages of local information. These information providers are true Free-Net and library partners. There are also over 6,381 links to Internet sites and most are to local information. Unlike some other Free-Nets, SEFLIN does not count links as SEFLIN information providers. The definition of a SEFLIN information provider is a group or individual who loads information on the SEFLIN Free-Net server.

In 1998–99, SEFLIN will also create a separate list and profile of Local Free-Net Linkers. It is a great accomplishment to empower 189 organizations; but we are aware there are many more groups in the region that need assistance. The process of assisting community groups to design, load and maintain quality web pages has been very labor intensive. It is fairly common for commercial Internet service providers to offer space for clients' web pages but few offer free training and ongoing support. Even agencies that offer workshops in the Internet, web and Hypertext Mark-up Language (HTML) do not provide free ongoing support to make the page a reality.

The SEFLIN Free-Net is a success on many, many levels. Usage is high, with over six million hits a year. The Free-Net serves both people in the region and others throughout the world. Local information is more accessible than ever before. The Free-Net has stimulated more cohesiveness in the community, and brought cooperation among libraries to a higher level than ever before. It has enhanced library visibility and established libraries as leaders in technology and collaboration. Through the Free-Net, SEFLIN libraries have demonstrated to the community that partnerships pay-off.

Perhaps the most important overall role for SEFLIN is to facilitate communication, which is essential for libraries to successfully work together and to share resources. There are many different ways to promote communication locally and regionally, including committee meetings, forums, showcases and special events, newsletters, brochures, the website, e-mail, discussion lists, regional calendars, etc. In the end, cooperation happens when people listen to each other, respect each other, and strive to understand each other. Partners must believe that greater results come from working together than from doing it alone. Partners must be able to see a vision and commit their energies to pursuing that common vision.

SEFLIN Values Statements

During its 1996 strategic planning session, the SEFLIN board of directors developed the following Values Statements, which guide the organization:

1. We believe that SEFLIN's leadership is a shared responsibility of all members. We are a member-driven organization that relies on the participation and initiative of every member of our organization to accomplish our shared goals.

2. We maintain and facilitate ongoing communication within the Southeast Florida library community.

3. We are committed to maintaining the strength of local library resources while developing new ways to expand the availability of those resources to the residents of Southeast Florida.

4. We recognize that SEFLIN's strength is dependent on the diverse nature of its members. We provide a strong committee structure that encourages our members to participate in planning and implementation.

5. We are committed to providing the best possible service to library customers through the development of innovative methods that result in new and effective library service.

SEFLIN Mission Statement

SEFLIN, a non-profit membership organization of Southeast Florida libraries, believes that libraries can make a difference in people's lives. Our mission is to work cooperatively with our members and the community to provide leadership, to promote sharing of library resources, to encourage joint use of technology and to support activities that enhance an individual library's ability to meet the informational, educational and cultural needs of their primary users and Southeast Florida residents. SEFLIN affirms the social value of libraries as key contributors to the community's social and economic well-being and quality of life. SEFLIN libraries provide the residents of Southeast Florida with links to local, state, regional and global information resources.

Florida Center for the Book

by Jean Trebbi
Executive Director
Florida Center for the Book

6

Introduction

The public library is often the only major cultural institution in many of the smaller communities in the U.S. It may provide space for lectures and exhibits, host concerts, or serve as the permanent address and meeting place for community historical societies and many other types of cultural organizations. This may also occur in larger cities, where an early commitment by a library to support specific cultural activities may continue on a permanent basis. Many libraries view the enhancement of cultural opportunity to the community as an essential element of their mission.

This chapter describes the steps that were initiated by the Broward County Library to fill a gap in the cultural activities available to its service population.

Background

The Florida Center for the Book (FCB) at Broward County Library (BCL) was established in 1984 as the first affiliate of the Center for the Book in the Library of Congress. It celebrates the literary heritage of Florida, brings readers and writers together, promotes books, reading, and libraries and acts as a catalyst and network for individuals and organizations interested in the book and encourages the development and expansion of the community of the book throughout Florida.

Broward County was largely unknown to the literary establishment. The Miami Book Fair had just been launched and Fort Lauderdale was best known for spring break. Sand castles were common beach construction sites, not a 250,000 square foot Main Library for Broward County that was beginning to fill most of its downtown block in Fort Lauderdale. While this Marcel Breuer-designed building was being completed, I wondered how the presence of this magnificent new building could help establish a presence for BCL both on the library and literary scene. What kind of accreditation could we earn to convey this?

As program coordinator for BCL, I had recently presented "Books that Make a Difference," a program initiated by the Library of Congress Center for the Book. The enthusiastic response from several communities prompted me to learn more about the Center for the Book in the Library of Congress.

Consulting the *U.S. Government Organization Manual*, I learned that the Center's mission complemented many of the libraries objectives. Conversations with key library staff and colleagues encouraged me to proceed with a proposal to the Library of Congress to establish an affiliation with the Center for the Book. John Y. Cole, Director of the Center, and his advisory board recommended it for approval. The library's designation as the first affiliate of the Center for the Book celebrated the 1984 dedication of Broward County's new Main Library. Since then, 30 state affiliates have been established and guidelines are available for libraries to apply for the distinction for the Center for the Book affiliate.

Partnership Notes
Type: Arts—Literary & Cultural
Services: Joint regional & statewide programs
Partner since: 1984

Figure 6.1: Florida Center for the Book logo.

Developing Partners

FCB's development since 1984 provides a good example of how Broward County Library leverages existing affiliations to attract new library users and secure higher levels of library support. Partnerships and networking have been keystones of the library since its establishment in 1974. In the ten years prior to the opening of the Main Library, useful literary linkages were developed, providing an expanding literary network. When Fred Ruffner, then president of Gale Research, founded The Council for Florida Libraries in 1979, the library was ready to help develop the council's mission of promoting public awareness of libraries statewide. Based in Fort Lauderdale, the council functioned as an umbrella organization of Friends of Libraries groups throughout the state, and contributed to the literary culture of Florida by providing technical assistance to its members through a book and author festival.

Book and Author Events

Book and author events were initially presented in eleven Florida cities, including Fort Lauderdale and grew in number as local libraries developed responsive audiences. The Key West Literary Seminar (KWLS) became one of the direct outgrowths of the festival. At that time in 1983, I had just started producing a local television program of author interviews called "Library Edition." While in Key West, I rented studio space and interviewed the authors participating in the seminar. Those authors also became prime candidates to participate in other literary programs.

The Day of Literary Lectures and Night of Literary Feast, now in its twelfth year, is an annual event presented by the library foundation. Every March approximately twenty authors donate a weekend of their time to present public lectures in the library and at local schools. They also become literary guests of honor at dinners in private Fort Lauderdale homes. The host donates the dinner, while guests dine with a favorite author for a contribution that benefits the Broward Public Library Foundation. Relationships have been established with guest writers who have been impressed by the local hospitality, arrangements and design of the program, especially the value they retained from the school visit. This helps build new audiences of readers and writers and engages students with distinguished authors. A volunteer committee of the foundation serves as literary escorts for a full weekend of activities. Lasting friendships and significant benefits can be traced to such events. Author Jeff Shaara convinced his family to gift the papers of his Pulitzer prize-winning father Michael, to the library's special collections and rare book department. Novelists Connie May Fowler, Olivia Goldsmith and Ben Bova have also donated manuscripts and papers, adding to this modern archive. FCB participates in securing authors for this event as well as others, such as the Palm Beach Bookfest and the annual Coral Springs Friends book and author luncheon. During the year, the phone frequently rings with the president of a Friends group requesting help to secure a speaker. FCB presents a monthly literary tea and author event in the cafe located within the Main Library. These afternoon teas have become increasingly popular and have drawn capacity audiences. Writing workshops, organized by FCB, are held in various library branches, and are presented for a half-day or in five-week segments. A published author lectures and engages would be writers, bringing the reader-writer relationship full circle.

Literary Landmarks Register

The network of partnerships expanded when the Literary Landmarks Register was founded, which is now a committee of Friends of Libraries USA (FOLUSA). Working with local partners, the FCB co-sponsored plaque dedications at such Florida literary sites as the homes or other locations linked to Elizabeth Bishop, Walter Farley, Robert Frost, John Hersey, Laura Riding Jackson, John D.

MacDonald, Jose Marti, Marjorie Kinnan Rawlings, Isaac Bashevis Singer, Wallace Stevens and Tennessee Williams. These designations enrich the literary landscape and help develop pride in Florida's literary heritage.

Unique Publications

The center's very first program set a literary standard when Pulitzer Prize-winning biographer Justin Kaplan presented a lecture at the library celebrating the 100th anniversary of Mark Twain's *Huckleberry Finn*. The lecture, "Born to Trouble," was frequently re-published jointly by the center and the Library of Congress, bringing significant attention to FCB nationally and internationally through broad distinction by the U.S. Information Agency.

"Let's Talk About It" was one of FCB's first off-site reading discussion series, which was presented in 25 libraries in Miami/Dade and Broward counties. Most of the program attendees were already "readers," but many were not previous library users. The program was later adopted by several other library systems, providing BCL & FCB with valuable statewide contacts. One of the books discussed in the series was *A Tan & Sandy Silence*, by John D. MacDonald. Originally issued in a limited edition as a fundraiser for both centers, it was subsequently republished by the Book-of-the-Month Club. More than fifty thousand copies were distributed. Through the generosity of Mrs. MacDonald, the proceeds from the reprint were shared by the Center for the Book in the Library of Congress and FCB. Publication opportunities have provided unexpected benefits and have helped to establish the literary reputation of BCL in general, and FCB in particular.

Celebrating a Year

When does a special year's celebration actually begin? In the case of the Year of the Young Reader," a new reading promotion of the Center of the Book, a designated day hadn't been established when I began exploring utilizing hospitals and birthing centers to distribute "Raise-a-Reader" kits. The image of hospitals connected with New Year babies. Those were the young readers you could actually reach on the first day of the Year of the Young Reader. The local newspaper crated a "Love Me, Read to Me" heart-shaped logo as a trademark, which was imprinted on baby T-shirts, included in the gift package with books, tapes and stickered on teddy bears. Broward Public Library Foundation registered the logo as a trademark and "Love Me, Read to Me" became a symbol for the library's children's programs. This national project celebrated a special year and brought visits from new parents to redeem coupons for copies of Jim Trelease's "Read Aloud Handbook," thus providing documented use of library users, particularly among new families.

Glorious Liaisons

New projects and programs are developed by recognizing new opportunities and resources. A link to the University of Miami led to a partnership involving the Historical Museum of Southern Florida to produce and host an exhibit project called "The Treasures of Florida's Libraries." Some 30 public and private institutions and collectors became partners by lending their unique and rare books, manuscripts, photographs and maps. Funding was provided by grants from SunBank, Social Issues Resources Series (SIRS), and the Southeast Florida Library Information Network, (SEFLIN). "Treasures of Florida Libraries" was featured at the American Library Association annual conference in Miami Beach in 1994 along with the scheduled pre-conference of the Rare Books and Manuscripts Section of the Association of College and Research Libraries. This brought local, regional, and national visitors to view items that had not been previously lent for exhibit before, including a leaf of the Gutenberg Bible, a papyrus fragment of an ancient Egyptian Book of the Dead,

Figure 6.2: *Treasures of Florida Libraries, presented at the Historical Museum of Southern Florida.*

Audubon's Birds, a Delius opera manuscript and George Washington's diary. A sense of renewed interest and appreciation for the collections emerged, and new support was developed for preservation, as well as for acquisitions in many local collections. The exhibit brought respect to Florida's libraries, with their treasured rare and unique materials, as well as local pride to the community.

Florida Literary Map

The expanded web of partners in the network of FCB and the new affiliates and partners of the Library of Congress Center for the Book has also expanded new national funding sources. The Lila Wallace-*Reader's Digest* Fund, for example, supported a major national Center for the Book project, "Language of the Land,' which celebrated the literary heritage of the states featuring literary maps from the Library of Congress collection. FCB presented the related exhibit in the Main Library's atrium drawing many visitors While touring in Florida, the exhibit was localized to solicit recommendations for a new map planned for Florida. Subsequently, the center received an award from the Florida Humanities Council to create and publish the map. The center steering committee took responsibility for the map's publication and reviewed design proposals. The published map describes the literary landscape of the entire state and its prize-winning authors, the places best associated with them, their prizes and prize-winning works, as well as Florida's Hall of Fame literary artists and literary landmarks. As a new literary resource the map has been well received, and distributed at major literary events, schools, colleges, universities, and public libraries. It has generated requests for copies in 50 states and beyond, from those interested in learning more about Florida's literary heritage.

Grants continue to fund literary projects, which are implemented by staff of the center, who are energetic and creative book lovers. The steering committee members, Broward Public Library Foundation, Friends of the Library groups, and other support staff at partnering libraries and organizations, have been essential to the success of FCB programs in Florida. A major grant proposal was presented to the Florida Department of State Division of Cultural Affairs to create new space within the Main Library for the literary arts—to mount exhibits, develop programs, present writing workshops and house rare books. An extraordinary award of $500,000 required a two-for-one match. The foundation donors provided the million-dollar match creating the Dianne and Michael Bienes Center for the Literary Arts in BCL, which opened in 1996 with the inaugural program presented by Poet Laureate Robert Hass.

Artists-in-Residence

The center has been able to develop model programs that offer in-depth literary experiences to our readers by continuing to forge new partnerships. Broward County Cultural Affairs Council presented an opportunity to joint venture in hosting an artist-in-residence. In a unique month-long residency, Irish playwright Maeve Ingoldsby worked with children's theater groups, and magnet schools. She lectured at the drama department of a local university, area school theater programs, and conducted story hours and storytelling workshops in Broward County libraries. Through these activities, she became a cultural catalyst galvanizing the Irish-American community, creating a new audience for the literary arts.

Figure 6.3: Florida Center for the Book and Broward residency of Irish playwright Maeve Ingoldsby.

Presence and Recognition

In 1996, BCL was chosen as *Library Journal's* Library of the Year, based on the outstanding partnerships it has developed in the community, state, and national levels.

The first Boorstin Center for the Book award was presented to FCB in recognition of its contribution to the Center for the Book's overall national program. The network of the Library of Congress and its resources are shared in ways that complement the interest and resources of local communities, enriching the experiences of readers and writers throughout the land.

Most recently, the Lila Wallace-*Reader's Digest* Fund invited the center to participate in a national "Audiences for Literature Network" along with six literary organizations recognized for their outstanding work. In response, the center has developed a series of literary programs for Fort Lauderdale, Venice and Orlando that will bring new and enriched literary experiences to Florida through 2001.

The original partnership establishing the Florida Center for the Book at BCL has enriched the literary community of the book, not only in Florida, but throughout the country, as other libraries from Alaska to Wyoming recognize a successful and viable model.

ArtServe

by Jennifer Carrigan Morrison
South Area Coordinator
Palm Beach County Library System

7

Partnership Notes
Type: Arts—Nonprofit
Services: Joint facilities
  and programs
Partner since: 1994

Many libraries have informal relationships with community arts organizations. Art shows, concerts, dramatic readings are regularly offered. Library bulletin boards are often crowded with posters and announcements promoting cultural events. Many surveys reveal that library users are more inclined to attend cultural events, so cooperative cultural programming represents marketing opportunity for arts organizations.

However, some libraries have gone farther than informal cooperative programming and publicity. Sharing facilities is one alternative that is less common, and there are pros and cons associated with it. This chapter describes the Broward County Public Library's experience in sharing facilities with a comprehensive arts organization.

Introduction

ArtServe's mission is to serve and strengthen the cultural community by providing leading edge facilities, training, professional consulting, technology and information services to individual artists, cultural groups and community stakeholders. ArtServe is a place where arts organizations pick up their mail, create and duplicate newsletters, and hold their monthly meetings. ArtServe is affordable office space for artists and cultural groups. It is an auditorium, a venue, a same day discount ticket booth, and a gallery as well as the service point of Volunteer Lawyers for the Arts (VLA) and Business Volunteers for the Arts (BVA). ArtServe is a partner of Broward County Library (BCL) and shares a building with the Fort Lauderdale Branch Library.

ArtServe helps not-for-profit cultural groups and individual artists with their business and administrative needs. There are offices and modular work stations available for rent to arts organizations with small staffs. There is a small meeting room that can be used for meetings with two to three people, larger rooms where monthly board meetings are held, and a computer room with word processing, spreadsheet and database software used to create newsletters and flyers, write grants, create and maintain mailing lists, and keep the books of cultural organizations. Printers and copier machines are available and copies can be made for a nominal charge. Fax machines, mail boxes, a message service and voice mail are provided to accommodate organizations without an office.

ArtServe encourages the growth of cultural organizations with educational and marketing programs. The "Arts Leadership Challenge" is a leadership training program designed to develop effective board members. Other educational opportunities include programs on marketing, copyright, organizational tools and legal issues. Business Volunteers for the Arts and Volunteer Lawyers for the Arts provide consulting services in nonprofit management basics, financial planning and reporting, board development, and long-range planning. The Broward Cultural Affairs Cooperative Marketing Program is administered by ArtServe. Advertisements for events and organizations are placed collectively in the local newspaper and other media. The marketing dollars are pooled and subsidized providing even small organizations the opportunity to reach a large audience.

Beth, a long time Fort Lauderdale Library patron, asks Anne Ruth at the reference desk, "What happened to the art?" Anne explains that the old show is over and the new art will be hung the next day. Shep Root, director of MONA (Museum of New Art), is nearby using the phone disc, art directories and local government directories to add to his mailing list. He overhears the conversation, looks up from his work and tells Beth about the new show, sponsored by his art organization. Beth listens and tells him what she liked about the old show and they talk about art for awhile.

45

ArtServe provides a venue. A beautiful gallery stretches the length of the building. Shows are developed by ArtServe staff using private support or member organizations can rent the gallery and develop their own shows. The auditorium seats over 200 and is used for performances, artist lectures, arts products seminars, film viewing and events. Same day discount ticket sales are available to many performances in the community.

The Broward County Library partners with ArtServe. It has developed a collection that supports ArtServe's mission. The building is maintained by the Library. The gallery, auditorium and other common areas are cleaned by the library's contract cleaners. ArtServe manages all of the meeting room space, booking and arranging the rooms and providing equipment. Library groups and staff committees use the space for meetings and library events. The resources of both organizations are shared and combined.

Figure 7.1: The Charlie Trainor Exhibit at ArtServe/Fort Lauderdale branch in July, 1997.

Background

The Fort Lauderdale Branch Library was once the large main library of the City of Fort Lauderdale. When the Broward County Library System was created, its role changed. In 1984, a new eight story Main Library was opened in the downtown business area. The government documents, periodicals, and extensive reference collection moved to the new Main Library. Along with the materials went eleven reference librarians, the audio-visual and periodical staff, and most of the circulation staff. Over the years, the Fort Lauderdale Library struggled to create a new identity. The library is located in the oldest residential area of the city and serves long-time influential citizens. The local community did not want to see the library changed, but with the Main Library only a mile and a half away, duplicating library services was not feasible. As the Main Library collection and staff grew, the services offered at the Main far surpassed any offered at the branch. Over time, the community embraced the new Main Library, but still clung to the old Fort Lauderdale Branch.

The branch struggled to maintain its former stature but reduced resources made it impossible. The budget decreased every year as the Main Library's grew. When staff received a promotion, or retired, their vacant position was moved to another location. After eight years, only half of the space created when it was a bustling research library was still being used. Monthly circulation figures had decreased to 8,000 per month. Building space was awkwardly arranged due to multiple renovations, and the facility was beginning to look dingy and seedy. The library, the collection, and the staff, all of which still reflected a main library mission that declining use did not support, needed a new role, new carpet, new walls, new roof—new everything. Closing it was not an option because it would deprive the neighborhood of a library it had used for 35 years.

Meanwhile, Business Volunteers for the Arts (BVA) was looking for a location. BVA provides arts organizations with business expertise in accounting, marketing, management, communications and planning support through a network of volunteer professionals. After reviewing requests from many arts organizations, these business leaders noticed that the same items appeared in most requests. Art and cultural organizations usually have limited financial resources and common needs. They need business tools—computers, copiers and other equipment—and basic business expertise to maintain and expand their artistic expression. Instead of funding each organization with money to buy duplicate equipment and services, BVA considered providing one common facility.

The Greater Fort Lauderdale Chamber of Commerce's Arts and Culture Subcommittee, Broward Cultural Affairs Council, and Broward County's Division of Cultural Affairs also recognized the common need and became involved in the proj-

David, a ten-year-old, is showing his mother color prints. He was forced to come to the program with his younger brothers. After listening to Cassandra Jones, Youth Services Librarian, tell the story "The Monkey People," an Art Guild instructor showed them how to make tissue paper collages. David had made his own monkey people with this illustration technique. He says to the branch manager, working the reference desk, "The library where we used to live had baby programs; this is better."

ect. Grants were secured from the National Endowment for the Arts, the State of Florida, and the Broward County Board of County Commissioners. Individual and corporate donations included substantial gifts from private donors Dianne and Michael Bienes, JM Family Enterprises and the Knight Foundation.

Having secured the community's support and major federal and state funding, all that was needed was a building to house the project. Several businesses donated temporary space but the project needed a permanent home. Constructing a new building or purchasing an existing building would consume too much of the available funds. The start-up money would help with the initial expenses, but not the costs of maintenance and utilities. Art and cultural organizations have limited operating funds. Frequently, underutilized space is made available for a reasonable sum, but utilities and maintenance costs are too expensive. Because these expenses would be prohibitive to most organizations, BVA began to look for existing space in a host institution.

The group didn't have far to look. The Division of Cultural Affairs once operated within Broward County Library's organizational structure and was aware of the dilemma about the future of the Fort Lauderdale Branch. Cultural Affairs Director Mary Becht sought suggestions from Library Director Samuel F. Morrison on the possibility of using space in the branch. Morrison quickly agreed that incorporating BVA into the underutilized space at the branch creatively addressed the needs of both organizations and provided the library with opportunities to reach new audiences, provide joint programming, and share valuable resources. An agreement was soon reached, contracts were signed, plans were drawn up, and the transition began.

The agreement was simple. ArtServe would lease space from the library for $1.00 per year and renovate the building according to plans approved by all parties. Any building improvements would belong to the county and library office space removed in the renovation would be replaced by ArtServe. The auditorium would be shared by both parties. ArtServe would manage the use of the auditorium but this important programming and meeting space would be shared.

The plans included a gallery that ran the length of the building, from the auditorium doors to the windows facing one of Broward's busiest streets—Sunrise Boulevard. The gallery would be tiled with terra cotta and would bridge the ArtServe and library areas. A zig-zag-shaped wall of windows defined the library area and glass fronted meeting rooms lined ArtServe's area.

Renovation

The Fort Lauderdale Library closed in December 1993. Patrons and staff were sent to the Main Library. Furnishings and the collection were boxed and stored. The building's interior was gutted and new walls, ceilings and floors were built. Giving up the space to ArtServe was not difficult.

Weekly construction meetings were held with ArtServe staff, the architect, county engineers, the contractor and library staff. The branch librarian was included in these meetings along with the east regional manager and the associate director for branch and regional services. Even though the funding for the project came from ArtServe and they administered the construction contracts, the library's interests were addressed.

Most of the meetings went smoothly with all concerned parties looking for solutions that would benefit both the library and ArtServe. For example, the original plans did not have floor to ceiling walls for the branch librarian and the east regional manager, and available resources were not sufficient to build new ceilings and carpeting for the entire building. The volunteer architect redrew the plans to the librarian's specifications and the contractor extended the walls. The Library Division and Cultural Affairs Division went to the Board of Broward County Commissioners and requested more money. It was granted. A concrete bench built into the wall outside the library entrance attracted panhandlers and substance abusers, and both library and BVA planners wanted it removed. This was a costly unbudgeted expense that could not be squeezed out of the construction budget. The County Facility Maintenance Division took care of it for the library. The public rest rooms were not budgeted for renovation because they were adequate and met Americans with Disabilities Act (ADA) requirements. They were, however, dingy and looked neglected. A local paint manufacturer who had donated all the interior paint for the renovation added a few more gallons to paint both rooms.

Both the library and ArtServe wanted to increase the building's visual presence. They wanted to take advantage of the fact that the building is located on a major east/west thoroughfare, and thousands of cars drive by each day. Renovation plans included a new facade with part of the original brick facade being covered with a stucco wave which was highlighted with neon-like fiber optics. Building designers felt new landscaping was needed to enhance the building's appearance, even though landscaping improvements were not in the budget. Local developer Roy Rogers of Arvida volunteered the "Green Team," a group of community volunteers that work to beautify Broward communities. The work was done on a Saturday morning by volunteers from the city with plants grown by the City of Fort Lauderdale Parks and Recreation Department, Broward County Parks and Recreation Department, and the Broward Chapter of Florida Nurserymen and Growers. The Green Team worked alongside city and county park employees, library staff and administration, members of the arts community, ArtServe staff and board members, and a group of juvenile offenders in a work program. Before lunch, hundreds of variegated liriope accented by pink pentas were planted.

The only construction problem arose over lighting. The contractor was only required to put in the same number of fixtures he removed. The branch librarian felt that the public areas of the library would be inadequately lighted and resources for additional fixtures had to be found. Both partners contributed to finding a workable compromise solution. The project electrician agreed to install the extra wiring at no additional cost and Broward County Library purchased the extra fixtures from their current year's operating budget. The problem was solved.

Preparing for Opening

As the building neared completion, however, operational problems arose and the auditorium was the battle ground. The agreement stated that ArtServe would schedule meetings and programs into the auditorium, their staff would set up and break down the room, and they would charge user fees to cover these costs—staff salaries, insurance, marketing, equipment and supplies—and generate revenue. Challenged with becoming self-supporting and anxious to survive financially, ArtServe felt it needed to severely limit the library's free use of the auditorium. A schedule was devised limiting the library's use of the auditorium to Wednesdays only and one night per month. Any other dates would have to be approved through a process so complicated, approval took six weeks. The library felt that it should continue using the library as it had prior to the closing. The large auditorium with free accessible parking and central location attracted quality programs. Author visits and other literary events that could not be accommodated by the Main Library were usually booked into the Fort Lauderdale Branch. Now the new process appeared so difficult that library staff feared it would be easier to book programs elsewhere.

Groups paying for the use of the auditorium frequently required access to kitchen facilities. The only kitchen was adjacent to the auditorium and served as the staff lounge. Library staff did not want to share the kitchen and their refrigerator with people who had rented the auditorium. ArtServe had a very small staff lounge only for their staff. Library staff and ArtServe members were not allowed to use the ArtServe staff lounge. In return, the library limited the use of its lounge to library staff only.

Sue Buzzi, the director of Broward Art Guild, is walking out of the building as Linda Jones from the Ashanti Cultural Arts is coming up the steps. The box of newsletters Sue has just finished duplicating are balanced on the hand rail while Sue and Linda talk about a program they want to do together—a mini art festival, using local visual and performing artists. Sue eventually leaves the newsletters with the library security guard and walks with Linda through the gallery to a hallway of offices. Linda unlocks the door to her office and Sue and Linda continue to plan the cooperative project.

During the construction stage, the partners looked for solutions together, and now as the opening day approached, the partners faced a number of challenges. The library needed to create a community role that satisfied long-time users and attracted new users. ArtServe had to develop a business support system that generated revenues that would allow it to operate with minimal outside funding. It needed to provide services to its members at cost, but at a cost the members could afford. Both organizations looked to the common resources as a means to reach those goals. Both saw that sharing these resources would be a problem. Rigid rules and procedures were developed, but they only created more barriers to cooperation.

Opening Day

The combined ArtServe/Fort Lauderdale Branch Library opened in September 1994. As the library support staff returned and ArtServe staff was hired, the partnership eroded to a less than peaceful coexistence. Territorial disputes festered. Library staff felt they and the library had been swallowed by ArtServe. The grand re-opening of the building was planned by and funded by ArtServe and the Division of Cultural Affairs. Library staff were made aware of the details. The opening day focused on ArtServe. Everyone who spoke, spoke about ArtServe. Mugs handed out to celebrate the opening only had ArtServe's name on it, not the library's. Local media covered the event but ignored the library. The library lived in the shadow of ArtServe. The opening of ArtServe was monumental. The Broward cultural community had charted new territory. There was nothing like it in the United States and other communities looked at it as a model. While opening any library is monumental, in 1994 the Broward County Library dedicated seven new or renovated libraries and this one seemed to have gotten lost among all the others.

Less Than Peaceful Coexistence

Library patrons complained about the new look, the art in the gallery, and the size of the library. Even though library staff loved the clean new look, the gallery filled with art, and the floor plan of the reduced library, the complaints became tiresome. A leaky roof in the public bathrooms that the county could not fix and a beautiful terra cotta floor that would not lay flat added to the discontent. The public men's room had to be shut, and patrons were directed to use the ArtServe staff rest rooms. The air conditioning was unreliable. ArtServe discontinued programming until the floor and roof were fixed. The gallery was empty. ArtServe and the Fort Lauderdale Branch operated side-by-side but not together. The partnership reached its lowest point.

Gradually things began to change. Leadership changes brought new perspectives and paying customers relieved some of the initial worries about funding. Staff members in both organizations found common ground and began developing programs in tandem. Member organizations began to move into the ArtServe office space. The Broward Art Guild, Theater for the Deaf, and Ashanti Cultural Arts became regular visitors in the library. They came into the library for information and relationships were formed. This developing cooperative spirit was celebrated at the first Winter Holiday Party recognized by the whole building. The Friends of the Fort Lauderdale Libraries provided the ham, ArtServe provided the turkey, and library staff and ArtServe staff and members each brought a dish. After the party, random acts of friendship and cooperation—helping carry packages, loaning coffee filters and cream, assistance in moving tables and chairs in the meeting room—became frequent. The frustrating building issues, a major cause of friction between the two staffs, were finally being addressed. The roof was replaced. The floor tiles continued to rise, but were glued back down promptly. The gallery was in use again.

The library patronage grew each month, but was only inching up to its pre-renovation figures. After being open for eight months, staff still heard patrons say "I

Figure 7.2: Invitation to the grand opening ceremony at ArtServe/Fort Lauderdale Branch Library.

didn't know you were open" and "I didn't know the library was still here, I thought it was an art center now." The east regional manager challenged the branch librarian to increase the circulation and the community's awareness of the library. The branch librarian drew on the resources of the library system for marketing and programming suggestions and planned a public open house to re-introduce the community to their branch library. To mitigate the singular and primary role ArtServe played at the opening day ceremonies, ArtServe staff provided support but were not active participants in the open house.

Eight hundred people came to the open house between the hours of 1–5 p.m.. It was an incredible success. The library and its staff were in the spotlight. For the first time since reopening, the library's identity was not overshadowed by ArtServe. The event boosted staff morale. ArtServe staff and members acknowledged the success of the event and wanted to be a part of the next event.

Improved internal communication generated by the success of the open house led to Broward Art Guild and the library developing a program "Telling a Story With Art." Cassandra Jones, the youth services librarian, tells a story, a guild art instructor teaches an illustration technique, and the children (from five to nine) illustrate the story. The Friends of the Fort Lauderdale Libraries funded the monthly program. Cooperative programming began.

ArtServe and the branch library developed a cooperative summer library program that included children's art in the gallery, dance, music and literary programs. ArtServe requested grant support from local corporate funds, but did not receive it. Using Friends funding again, part of the program was implemented, using member dance, film and arts groups. In the fall, the second annual Open House featured ArtServe, ArtServe member organizations, and the library. Nine ArtServe members participated by providing free performances, film viewing and activity booths. ArtServe staff helped handle the auditorium set-ups and sound system. Other ArtServe members assisted the library staff at activity tables, making newspaper hats, tissue paper flowers and blowing up balloons. Again, the Friends supported the event and staff from the Main Library assisted in library card registrations and charging out materials. And again, over eight hundred people attended, this time recognizing the building and its unique partnership.

The Future

The ArtServe/Fort Lauderdale Branch Library began as a partnership of convenience. The potential for dynamic programming was there from the beginning, but it took time to develop. ArtServe and the library operated apart from each other in the beginning. Staff on all levels should have been involved in the renovation project. Common staff areas should have been included in the plans. Formalized plans for cooperative programming and appropriate marketing of the partnership should have been incorporated earlier. Regular meetings between the staffs of the two organizations, an exchange of representatives on each partner's board of directors, and shared social events have improved communication and the long-term potential for a successful partnership. The ArtServe/Fort Lauderdale Branch Library building is now a place where arts organizations and the community meet together, to get a book, to look at art, to see a performance, and to get information. They share a library and a cultural experience. The two organizations now share a more fully defined and workable commitment to build future audiences of arts and library patrons.

Partnerships in the Lively Arts

by Sherry Lynch
Assistant Director/Community Relations & Partnership Development

Tanya Simons-Oparah
Assistant Director/Outreach Services

Cultural programming in the public library is recognized as a means to attract both adults and children into the institution, and an effective way to market or showcase the library's cultural resources. However, the cost of obtaining good quality programming, such as a chamber music ensemble, a dramatic production, or a modern dance troupe, can be sobering. When the cost of the talent is coupled with the expense for publicity and staging, most libraries turn to lesser alternatives.

There are organizations and sponsors, however, who would welcome the opportunity to partner with a library in planning more ambitious cultural programming because library users represent a new potential market. The development of young audiences is another major objective of many cultural organizations. This chapter describes several successful cooperative programs that benefited the library, the cultural group, and the community.

Broward County's rich cultural environment offers the library many varied partnership opportunities with cultural and performing arts organizations. Broward's Main Library, even in the planning stages, was considered a key cultural institution. When business and civic leaders in Broward began "plotting the transformation of the downtown core in Fort Lauderdale in the mid 1970s, it was their intention to make downtown a center of culture with a county library (Main opened in 1984), an art museum (completed in 1986), a performing arts center (completed in 1991)."[1]

Emphasizing the library as a cultural institution in conjunction with cultural colleagues has enabled BCL to highlight other less emphasized facets of the library's resources—our multi-formatted fine arts collection, performance spaces, and an environment conducive to everyone's creative, imaginative thoughts and ideas.

Partnership Notes
Type: Arts—Performance
Services: Joint programs
Partners since: 1994

Broadway at the Library

In association with the Florida Theatrical Association, Florida Philharmonic, and Broward Center for the Performing Arts, BCL has been able to introduce many new audiences of people to the library. In 1994 BCL was invited to become a partner with the Florida Theatrical Association (FTA) for the purpose of helping the public learn more about Broadway through a free program called *Discover Broadway at the Main Library*. Led by a central moderator, these programs offered the public an opportunity to explore theater from the perspective of actor, critic, director, and audience. FTA's education director, Kevin Keegan, proposed the idea for an interactive program at the library because he felt it was important to "utilize the resources from national Broadway touring shows to help educate students, teachers and the general public."

Carol Lawrence and author Lois Wise, in *Funny You Don't Look Like a Grandmother,* launched the series in a corner of Main Library's Fine Arts Department. From there, the series grew into larger space as word spread that the public could interact with Broadway casts and

Figure 8.1: *The Discover Broadway at the Library Series, sponsored by the Florida Theatrical Association, presents the cast and crews of nationally touring Broadway shows to the general public.*

crew members. Some wonderful comments about libraries have surfaced, like the one from Linda Balgord who played the role of Norma Desmond in *Sunset Boulevard*. When asked how she became an actress, Ms Balgord stated that she got her start in her local library! Her hometown librarian turned to the willing teenager for help when she needed someone to lead the children's story hour. Linda Balgord loved the roles she played in the New Lisbon Public Library so much that she decided to be an actress. When BCL began the practice of giving VIP library cards to cast members, Lois Markle, a member of the cast in *Three Tall Women*, was so happy with her card that she requested them at the other library sites in Florida where the production appeared. VIP cards are now given at every library site in Florida.

Each new show offers BCL new opportunities. When the hit production of *Stomp* was still on Broadway, the first national touring company was previewed for the South Florida media on the Main Library's outdoor plaza. Library Director Samuel F. Morrison and a group of New York cast members demonstrated the rhythm and beat of oil drums, brooms, and other unlikely props. Following his performance, Morrison shared with the media that "the library is proud to offer this new program in cooperation with the Acura Broadway Series ... through partnerships like this, the general public can learn about the many educational resources available in Broward County."

BCL receives acknowledgment for its support of the series in approximately 26,000 programs distributed each week during a production. *Introduction to Broadway at the Library* is also described in each edition of *Encore!*, a marketing brochure which goes to all local season ticket subscribers. Information on the BCL/FTA partnership and has been prominently featured in *Broadway Presents*, a trade publication published by Celebrate Broadway, Inc. as a joint venture of The League of American Theaters and Producers and Playbill, Inc. Beginning in 1995, BCL's program model was replicated by public libraries in Miami/Dade, Palm Beach, Orlando and Tampa.

Over time this successful program has grown and evolved to meet the changing needs of FTA, the library, and our audiences. In the early years, cast members were interviewed by a local cable TV personality and actress, Iris Acker, for her program *On Stage with Iris Acker*. Today's moderators are local radio and TV personalities and the sessions are not taped. Participants have learned to expect the unexpected and seem to look forward to the possibilities of "chance happenings." Often the names of the cast members to be interviewed aren't known until the morning of the program or one actor is substituted for another. From time to time participants are late and once a program was cancelled at the last moment because an extra rehearsal was needed. The opportunity to gain an insider's perspective of what goes on behind the scenes of a Broadway production has increased audiences for both partners, and both feel *Introduction to Broadway at the Library* has had a successful five-year run.

Beach, the Library & Beethoven

During the summer of 1997, *Beethoven by the Beach* became Broward's first cultural tourism initiative, bringing together the community's major cultural institutions—the Florida Philharmonic, Broward Center for the Performing Arts, Florida Grand Opera, Fort Lauderdale International Film Festival, Museum of Art, Museum of Discovery & Science, and BCL.

Under the leadership of the Florida Philharmonic (FP)—the state's largest performing arts organization serving a region populated by more than four million people—Broward's first-ever summer festival of music and art included performances of all of the Beethoven symphonies and piano sonatas, as well as the highly acclaimed children's program, *Beethoven Lives Upstairs*, open rehearsals, chamber concerts, renowned guest artists, movies, lectures and symposiums, throughout all of Fort Lauderdale's downtown Arts & Science District.

Figure 8.2: Beethoven by the Beach invited residents and visitors to concerts, lectures, movies, and children's programming during a twenty-day-long festival.

The festival gained local, regional, national and international attention and exposure for Broward and the cultural partners. Travel and leisure industry publications, international publications such as Britain's *BBC Breadth • Depth • Opinion Magazine* and Argentina's *Clasica Radio* and the *New York Times* all carried stories about Broward's summer music festival.

This was not the first time that BCL has been affiliated with the Florida Philharmonic and the other partners. For example, over the past dozen years members of the FP have presented Luncheon Music Talks to members of the Broward Public Library Foundation and programs for young people at special library events like the Children's Reading Festival. This was, however, the first time that a project of such magnitude was undertaken cooperatively by all of Broward's major cultural institutions.

Over the twenty days of the festival more than 1,600 people—locals and tourists—attended "Sonata-thon" and "Camp Beethoven" programs in BCL's Main Library. The *Herald*'s music critic, James Roos, declared that "Judging from the large crowds at most concerts, this festival may be the catalyst that forever transforms South Florida's summer concert scene ... concerts were jam-packed mainly with new customers." The library was able to showcase both our performance spaces, and the resources available in our collection and our Youth Services Department.

Favorable public response to the library's participation in *Beethoven by the Beach* gave the library the chance to play a leadership role in designing programs and projects for upcoming festivals.

> **Rising Star Camp Objectives**
> - provide relevant role models
> - develop specific, measurable physical, analytical and artistic skills
> - encourage positive peer recognition
> - provide opportunities for community participation
> - provide model for others to replicate

Stars Rise at the Library

Building relationships with partners one project at a time, such as the library foundation's Luncheon Music Talks and the Children's Reading Festival with the Florida Philharmonic, opened the door to *Beethoven by the Beach*. Similarly, the library's long-term affiliations with the Broward Center for the Performing Arts resulted in the new Rising Stars Summer Theater Camp for ten- to fourteen-year-olds.

In the summer of 1996, the BCPA initiated the Rising Stars Summer Theater Camp in a free cooperative venture with the library. The camp was intended as a model summer day camp designed to enhance the self-esteem, creative expression and analytical skills of middle school youngsters from Broward's underserved communities. The mission of Rising Stars is to provide a positive learning experience to ten- to fourteen-year-olds before they enter high school.

The initial six-week camp (July 8–August 14, 1997) for 50 youths was held at the BCPA and at three of BCL's branches. The class schedule ran from Monday through Wednesday, and it included dance technique classes (alternating between ballet, modern jazz and tap), acting classes, music and drama classes, theater business classes and library skills and research classes. Campers also produced their own show and starred in an end-of-camp performance for family and friends at the BPAC.

The strength of this partnership is mutually shared goals. The library was interested in involving community children who were not trained in the arts and might be lost to the streets or left home alone. The BCPA wanted to create a relationship with youth in a nonschool atmosphere centered around learning about the arts as a career possibility and developing an enjoyment for the arts as entertainment. Both partners were interested in increasing their customer bases. In the future, measurable data will be collected which will reflect the value and impact of the program on the children, their communities and the library. This documentation is an important step in seeking new partners and support.

Figure 8.3: Flyer for the Rising Stars Summer Theater Library Camp.

Notes

1. *The Herald*, "The Downtown Renaissance," Monday, December 15, 1997.

Partners for Children

by Marlene Lee
Youth Services Coordinator
Broward County Library

9

Partnership Notes
Type: Children & Youth
Services: Joint programs
Partners since: 1986

Ever since public library service to children became accepted practice, youth services librarians have sought creative ways to attract children, and to stimulate their interest in reading and learning. Historically, these programs were basic and they relied primarily upon resources that were available in the library, such as preschool story hours, and simple craft projects using supplies drawn from the library's supply closet. Often, reading incentives and special supplies were purchased out of the librarians' own pockets, since the allocation of funds for creative youth programming and promotion was slow to gain acceptance. Even today, many youth services staff have limited funds for special programming such as professional storytellers, incentives for summer reading programs, and opportunity for outreach to groups such as economically disadvantaged children.

Because of their dedication, many youth librarians have found alternative funding through a combination of public and private partnerships to permit them to offer a wide variety of programs for youth. Often the sources of funding are as innovative as the creative services and programs they support. This chapter illustrates how the library can apply the principles of partnership in developing and sustaining an award-winning array of youth services and programs.

For more than a decade, corporations and community organizations have joined forces with Broward County Library (BCL) youth services, through the library foundation, to bring children quality programming and expanded collections. These partnerships have helped to fill the needs of the community and have contributed to the missions of these agencies.

Figure 9.1: Bert Bear and friend visit with area children.

Bert Harmon, Partner and Friend

Partnerships between libraries and corporations or organizations often grow from the passion of one person to serve a specific group. Bert Harmon, children's advocate and former library advisory board member, was one such exceptional person. In 1986, Mr. Harmon funded the first "Conference on Children's Literature," a full day of programs featuring authors and storytellers, which is now held every spring prior to our annual Children's Reading Festival. In 1987, Mr. Harmon also initiated a new annual program for preschoolers. Every December, "Books and Bears at the Holidays" provides an invitation to hundreds of children from daycare centers in low-income areas to come to local neighborhood libraries for a holiday program and the gift of a bear and a book. Bert Bear, a costumed character who hosts the annual event, embodies Mr. Harmon's generous spirit.

The Books and Bears program has been underwritten by Mr. Harmon for several years. After those years of Harmon funding, the Broward Public Library Foundation, a nonprofit organization whose mission is to "make a good library great," secured the sponsorship of the Miami Herald for an additional several years.

Partnerships often result in benefits greater than the sum of the collaborative efforts. Following are some comments from senior volunteers about their experience reading to under-served children in area day care facilities:
"I can't wait till Tuesdays when I do story time at the day care center."
"If I knew I was going to have this much fun after retirement, I would have retired sooner."
"I miss my grandchildren terribly. Now I have twenty children to hug and kiss each week."

Primetime: A partnership with the A.D. Henderson Foundation

For the past four years, nearly 300 seniors have volunteered to deliver the popular "Prime Time" storytelling program to 85 daycare centers. Prime Time pairs preschool children with seniors who commit to providing ten story times at their assigned daycare center. Numbered story kits, in heavy canvas bags with the Prime Time logo, are stationed at branch libraries close to the daycare centers. There are one hundred kits with ten themes—enough for a different half-hour story time each week. Each kit contains age-appropriate books, props, song sheets, finger plays and hand stamps. Volunteers pick up their kits a day prior to a scheduled program so that they have time to practice. After their storytime program, the volunteer returns the kit to the library for the next volunteer.

Figure 9.2: Prime Time, an intergenerational program funded by the A.D. Henderson Foundation, transforms senior citizen volunteers into animated storytellers for disadvantaged children.

After ten weeks, volunteers are encouraged to continue on their own, with guidance from youth services librarians. Many do. Some volunteers, who have been reading for as long as four years, attend beginners' training sessions to share their enthusiasm. Everyone wins: children make seniors feel wanted and needed; senior volunteers shower attention on preschoolers who may live far from their own grandparents. Senior volunteers agree that introducing children to books and reading is very rewarding. The library benefits by developing library users—both young and old.

Prime Time Guidelines

1. Call the director or contact person at the preschool facility assigned to you to get directions to the school, and to determine a mutually convenient day and time for your story program, beginning the week of January 5 (or earlier, if you just can't wait!).

2. Call program coordinator, and leave a message about your agreed upon story time.

3. Visit your assigned Prime Time library location and pick up a story kit before you visit your preschool site. You may want to pick up the kit a couple of days before your story time, to become familiar with the contents of the kit.

4. Keep a record of story kit usage on the enclosed sheet in this notebook, to avoid duplicating story programs.

5. All Prime Time volunteers are expected to complete ten hours of service at their assigned preschool site. See enclosed Prime Time Calendar. Any missed story times may be rescheduled at the convenience of the school and the volunteer.

6. Fill out the Prime Time Log sheet, which is located in this notebook, at each visit to the school. this is our only record of your service.

7. Return the story kit to your assigned library as soon as possible after your story program, as other Prime Time volunteers are waiting for it.

8. Have fun!

9. After finishing your ten story programs, your formal commitment to Prime Time has been fulfilled. We hope that you will have found the experience rewarding, and will want to continue bringing story programs to preschoolers. If so, you may continue weekly visits to your center for as long as you like, or you may contact program coordinator to request reassignment to a different center. In either case, you may reuse the same ten story kits (children like and learn from the repetition of favorite stories), or you may create your own story programs. Your local children's librarian can help you select books.

In 1991, Mary Somerville, past president of the American Library Association (ALA) and former BCL youth services coordinator, wrote a federal Library Services and Construction Act (LSCA) grant proposal which provided $45,700 to start Prime Time. The grant provided funds for a coordinator, clerical assistants, books, realia and training materials. Part of the funding sent a delegate to the 1993 ALA annual conference in San Francisco to explain the program to an inter-generational caucus.

Three months after the grant was awarded, Shelly Turetzky was hired as administrator. Shelly's energy and enthusiasm set the standard for the Prime Time program. She canvassed condominiums for volunteers and advertised in a variety of publications with great success.

Jo Bridges, a local professional storyteller, working as a consultant, purchased materials and organized story kits. She developed training manuals, and provided the initial half-day training sessions that prepared volunteers to read effectively to preschoolers. Each trained volunteer was then assigned to a federally subsidized day-care center.

Following the departure of the original grant administrator, Katy Mullon, a special events coordinator for our youth services department, added Prime Time to her already long list of responsibilities. She regrouped youth services librarians to train volunteers, recycled books and bags, and rounded up volunteers to make phone calls and provide clerical support.

Katy now runs two Prime Time series each year and has more people who want to volunteer than materials to give them or time to train them. About 35 percent of the volunteers continue in the program from year to year.

Sustaining the funding for Prime Time presents a challenge. After the initial grant, the Broward Public Library Foundation arranged for new sponsorships to provide some limited funding. American Express and J. C. Penney were sponsors for a short time. While it operates on a shoestring, the program has won two awards. In 1997, Highsmith Inc. bestowed its Award of Excellence on BCL's Prime Time program, which included a $1,000 grant. Additional funding came in the form of a memorial for a Prime Time volunteer. His family said the program brought him so much joy that he read at three centers, in addition to the one he was assigned. In 1995, the program won the NACo (National Association of Counties) Achievement Award for significant innovative activities that improve the services of counties.

Read 'n' Ride: A partnership with the Broward County Fair

The Broward County Fair has always offered free admission to children with school identification cards on designated days. Fair officials agreed to extend free admission to children with library cards. Additionally, children who completed an eight-book reading log could enjoy one ride free. Up to three reading logs could be accepted. Since admission to the fair is $5 and rides can be as much as $3, these were powerful incentives. Also, each of BCL's 33 branches holds a drawing. The winner gets a Family Packet, which is free admission for the entire family, ride tickets and T-shirts. The Fair includes BCL in its advertising, prints the reading logs, and provides all the incentives. The Library distributes the logs, provides publicity by displaying posters and distributing flyers. Broward County Schools encourage participation by distributing the reading logs through their media centers.

Books and Bats: A partnership with the Florida Marlins

For libraries in or near metropolitan areas with sports teams, partnership with these clubs is popular. Broward, Miami-Dade and Palm Beach Counties are partners with the Florida Marlins baseball team, winners of the 1997 World Series. Each summer, as a bonus to the summer library program, participating children who read ten books are eligible for two admission tickets to a Marlins' game in August. The program

---

Obstacles to avoid in developing intergenerational programs:

- Pairing seniors with centers which are long distances from home or are in unfamiliar neighborhoods.

- Volunteers who are unprepared for cultural and social differences.

- Health risks.

Recommended solutions:

- Make every effort to be sure the volunteer is content with his or her assignment.

- Enlist a local social agency to explain the cultural and social differences volunteers might encounter.

- Arrange for flu shots with the local health department.

begins in May with Librarians' Night at the Ballpark. Library administrators from the three counties promote libraries and reading during the pregame activities on the field. In addition to tickets, Marlins provide enough bookmarks and posters for all library branches. The team's mascot, Billy the Marlin, appears at library events during the summer.

BCL's program started because Paula Coy, a youth services librarian and avid baseball fan, regularly enjoyed the games of a small community team called the Pompano Miracles. Through her friendship with the team's promoter, the library was offered free admission tickets. Librarians were enthusiastic attendees and their loyalty was noted. When the Florida Marlins came to South Florida, the Miracles promoter joined the Marlins marketing team. He approached his library friends with the offer of tickets and soon a tri-county (Broward, Miami-Dade and Palm Beach) partnership was born.

Children are highly motivated to read by this program and look forward to it every summer. Challenges with the program do occur, however, and once the decision is made about the deadline for reading ten books and the allotment of tickets for each branch and the game date set, there are still hurdles to overcome. Faithful readers discover the game date is during their vacation week, affluent patrons are disappointed with the location of their seats, and others can't afford transportation and parking fees at the ballpark. While the solutions to the first two items remain unresolved, the transportation situation has been addressed with the local chapters of the Urban League and Boys and Girls Clubs providing bus transportation to the ballpark.

Folke H. Peterson Charitable Foundation

In 1993, the Folke H. Peterson Charitable Foundation, which is dedicated to education about and protection of Florida wildlife, approached the Broward Public Library Foundation, seeking a partnership with the library. The Foundation offered to donate funds for books and materials if the library acted as repository and conduit to the public. The partnership was accepted, and in the first two years, all branch libraries and the bookmobile received programs, exhibits and books. In the third year, computer kiosks were installed in eight libraries, with plans to add two more installations each year. Each terminal has six interactive CDs about endangered nature and wildlife.

In 1997, the Peterson Foundation created two high-quality videos: *Coexisting with Wildlife* and *Creating a Backyard Habitat* which were distributed to all branch libraries. Because of the quality of the videos, Eileen Cobb, BCL's associate director of branch and regional libraries, and a recent president of the Florida Library Association, proposed a project to the FLA Board: to share the two videos about Florida wildlife with all Florida libraries free of charge. Since the Foundation held the copyright, it made the copies and sent them to every library in Florida at no expense to the Florida Library Association.

Children's Reading Festival: *An event with multiple partners*

The highlight event of the year in BCL's Youth Services program is the Children's Reading Festival, a three-day event held every spring for the last nine years in cooperation with the Broward Public Library Foundation. It remains the only free downtown cultural event for children. Held in and around the Main Library, an eight-story building overlooking Stranahan Park, the festival celebrates books and reading by bringing stories to life. Twenty thousand children and parents come out to see marionettes, magicians, storytellers and costumed characters from literature, ballet, symphony and theater. Four stages and an historical storytelling house feature simultaneous performances. Tents with craft supplies are staffed by volunteers who help children make such things as paper hats, finger puppets and sand sculptures.

The planning and coordination for this go on for almost the entire year. Youth services librarians cut and assemble craft materials for the arts and crafts tent. Staff scouts children's festivals for talent. The vendor chairperson interviews food vendors and tests the quality of the products they offer. The two-day festival is held on a Saturday and Sunday in April and requires the efforts of over 200 community volunteers (mostly teens) and all 55 youth services librarians.

On the Friday of the festival weekend, the Conference on Children's Literature is offered to librarians, educators and interested public. Outstanding authors, illustrators and storytellers provide a full day of lectures and workshops. Attendees from as far away as Jamaica have participated.

Originally, the festival was developed by the library in league with the Sun-Sentinel newspaper and Florida Center for the Book, which was celebrating "The Year of the Young Reader" in 1989. Today, these events, including the professional day, are sponsored by corporations such as Blockbuster, the Sun-Sentinel, NationsBank, Motorola, Channel 4, American Express, and the North Broward Hospital District, as well as various foundations and civic groups. Through the efforts of Kay Harvey, Executive Director of the Broward Public Library Foundation, corporations donate through the Foundation for events such as the festival. She often directs them to a specific activity such as the Storytelling House or a craft tent. Performance stages bear sponsors' names. The Sun-Sentinel runs large advertisements as far as a month in advance. These ads are an example of the type of in-kind support that the festival receives. Because the library cannot afford to purchase the quality or quantity of publicity it gets from the Sun-Sentinel, it judiciously accepts support that has significant benefit to the library and meets certain standards. Products which are harmful to children are excluded. Companies seeking self-promotion or free publicity through the library are not considered potential partners.

Most recently, a new sponsor, the A.D. Henderson Foundation, has enabled us to give a free book to children who attend the Reading Festival. Coupons to be redeemed at the Festival's Great Book Giveaway are available at retail shops and at libraries.

Conclusion

In the past the only source of funds to support special library events for youth was provided by the Library Friends' groups. Due to our successful partnerships, children in all of Broward County's libraries, whether they have strong individual support from their Friends' groups or not, can enjoy special events and programs. For this reason, we continue to pursue partners for new opportunities.

Small Business Resource Center

by Shirley Amore
Director
Sarasota County Libraries

Partnership Notes
Type: Business/Corporate
Services: Joint programs
 & services
Partners since: 1995

Libraries have gained considerable experience in developing partnerships with other nonprofit organizations and agencies. Their experience in partnerships with the for-profit sector, however, is more limited. Many libraries have sought corporate sponsorship of library programs, but few have gone beyond this to cooperatively develop and implement major projects in conjunction with a corporate partner. The Broward County Library/NationsBank Small Business Resource Center provides a case study to illustrate the advantages as well as some of the challenges to keep in mind when forging such a relationship.

Background

A few years ago, BCL Director Samuel F. Morrison realized the need to provide targeted service to the small business community at the Main Library in downtown Fort Lauderdale. He was keenly aware of the high failure rate of new businesses and the importance of a healthy small business community to the overall health of the local economy. He knew that the library could provide the information these businesses needed to become successful. He also visualized the library as a bridge between the business community and governmental agencies, and saw an opportunity to coordinate and streamline services to this clientele. He particularly wanted to reach minority and women business owners. He shared his vision with the library staff and challenged them to come up with a plan to accomplish this goal.

The staff responded by strengthening the small business collection, producing bibliographies on specific small business topics and increasing outreach to the small business community. This included working more closely with the Senior Corps of Retired Executives (SCORE) and the Florida Atlantic University Small Business Development Center to provide programs at the library. Library staff actively participated by conducting workshops and tours highlighting important business resources available at the Main Library.

With the help of a $10,000 grant from the City of Fort Lauderdale, staff produced an attractive and colorful brochure describing the many resources and services for the business community available at the library. The brochure included a response card that could be returned to the library to receive more information on specific business topics. This project allowed the staff to develop a mailing list for future programs and services—and to tailor the collection and services to meet the needs and interests of the community. The brochure was widely distributed, and it increased community awareness of the Main Library and its extensive small business collection.

In 1995, Mr. Morrison asked the library foundation to help with this project. Letters were sent to local corporations inviting them to work with the library to expand the scope of the project. The library director and the executive director of the foundation were successful in recruiting James Cassady, senior banking executive of NationsBank. Because Mr. Cassady was a member of the library foundation board,

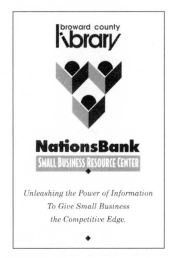

Figure 10.1: Small Business Resource Center logo.

he already had an interest in helping the library. The Main Library director and the executive director of the library foundation made a presentation to the staff of NationsBank outlining the library's plans for a small business resource center. The presentation struck a nerve with the NationsBank staff since the bank had recently developed free-standing small business resource centers in some of their market areas. The idea of partnering with a library to provide this service particularly appealed to them. With the blessing of all parties involved, a partnership was born.

Getting Started

All parties came to the table filled with enthusiasm for the project. It took a while to realize that we had different ideas and expectations of the Small Business Resource Center. In retrospect, this shouldn't have come as any great surprise, since we were approaching the project with different missions and philosophies. And, as a result of these differences, we continually needed to clarify our expectations for the center throughout the planning process.

The first order of business was to assemble an implementation team. The Main Library director, the executive director of the library foundation and the vice president for community investment from NationsBank spearheaded the effort. Separate task forces composed of staff from the library and the bank were assigned to work on different pieces of the plan. The most important step in the process was the development of a formal agreement that clearly spelled out the goals and expectations of each party, including the scope, the responsibilities of each party and the budget for the project. (See page 79 for information about appendices on the Highsmith Press website, including the NationsBank agreement with Broward County and the Broward County Public Library Foundation.)

The parties agreed on the following mission statement for the Small Business Resource Center (SBRC):

"The mission of the SBRC is to provide the best possible small business assistance through resource materials, training, counseling and technical support, producing the optimum potential for small business success in this community."

In defining the scope of the project, it was very helpful that NationsBank already had some experience with small business resource centers. We were also lucky to have the person who designed the original resource center in Nashville as a consultant.

What is the Nashville model? The NationsBank Small Business Resource Center in Nashville opened in 1992. It was designed to be a one stop shopping destination for small business people in the community. NationsBank partnered with the Small Business Administration and other governmental agencies to provide help in the form of information, resources, assistance, education, training and counseling. The key subject areas of the collection are planning, accounting, management, finance, marketing and personnel. Resources are provided in a focused and guided approach with self-help and hands-on formats. Assistance, education, training, and counseling are provided by sponsors and local supporters of the center. In addition to supplying at no charge the latest small business resource materials and state of the art technology, the center works with other organizations to supply small business assistance programs to the community. The center serves as a conduit through which various entities desiring to help small business offer their services and programs. A primary goal of the Nashville center is to provide the synergy and efficiency of an unique delivery system to bring together a wide range of small business assistance programs. NationsBank has since developed other centers in cities where NationsBank has a presence, all using this very successful model. It quickly became clear to all parties that the Nashville concept could work very successfully in a library setting. All parties agreed to adopt the Nashville model for this project.

The parties further agreed that the center would be located on the fifth floor of the Main Library in the Business, Law and Government Department and that the primary service area would be Broward County with a secondary service area to include the contiguous counties of Palm Beach and Miami-Dade. The agreement clearly stated that BCL would be responsible for the day-to-day management of the small business resource center and that full-time staffing of the SBRC would be provided, compensated and controlled by the library.

Library Foundation Goals

Spelling out the expectations and areas of responsibility was critical to the success of the project. The goals of the library foundation, working through BCL, were to provide the information, resources and educational tools to meet the needs of small businesses in Broward County and to provide easy access and a more focused, proactive system for assisting small businesses. The foundation and library expected that the small business resource center would:

- Serve as the central reference point that small and emerging businesses turn to first to fill their information needs.

- Become the most accessible clearinghouse for small business information and government resources in Broward County.

- Have an up-to-date reference library of business materials in print, audio, video and computer formats.

- Serve as a location to access supplemental materials in the Broward County Library System and other major libraries in South Florida and across the country.

- Function as a gateway to the Internet.

- Provide objective small business information efficiently and confidentially.

- Become a source of continuing education via corporate, educational and civic organizations geared to the individual's specific business needs.

- Become a constant supplier of ongoing workshops and seminars on business development and specific small business topics.

Library Foundation Support

The library and foundation agreed to support the small business resource center in the following ways:

- Provide space on the fifth floor of the Main Library to the center at no cost.

- Absorb all utilities, maintenance, insurance and telecommunications expenses.

- Make available existing and newly acquired resource materials including print and audiovisual, as well as computer databases and network access.

- Provide a full-time library specialist I.

- Provide additional in-kind administrative support.

- Provide six computers and six printers.

- Provide full cooperation of library staff in supporting the functions and activities of the SBRC as it relates to their areas of responsibility.

- Recruit volunteers to provide counseling in the SBRC.

- Assist in conducting joint workshops.

- Recruit financial support (in kind and cash).

- Provide library-developed information and literature.

- Work with co-sponsors on special projects and initiatives.

- Utilize SBRC to enhance the Library's new and existing programs.

- Market the SBRC and its usage through all appropriate methods.

NationsBank Goals

NationsBank's goal in sponsoring the SBRC was to create a small business resource center that would provide meaningful, beneficial, tangible and measurable results in assisting small businesses in the area. By providing a unique mechanism to deliver efficient and professional assistance to small business, NationsBank expected to provide more products and services to the small business community, especially minority and underserved markets. In other words, the bank expected to increase its bottom line as well as provide an important community resource. NationsBank saw the SBRC as:

- The focal point of all small business assistance efforts in the community.
- A source of information and assistance about government guaranteed loan programs.
- An intake facility for various funding programs.
- A primary location for teaching the NationsBank Small Business Success sessions.
- The primary information center to promote all beneficial small business assistance programs in the area.
- The referral location for all clients needing assistance with business planning.
- A facility open to the entire community for use in the promotion of small business success.
- Not just a physical location to assist small business, but a concept and philosophy of providing a more effective way for organizations, whose purpose it is to assist small business, to get their beneficial services to the small business entrepreneur.

NationsBank Support

NationsBank agreed to support the SBRC by:

- Providing cash funding in the total amount of $150,000 ($30,000 per year over a five year period).
- Providing funding for a librarian II to manage the SBRC.
- Facilitating the entire project development based on the small business resource center model developed by NationsBank.
- Providing marketing and public relations support.
- Planning, funding and implementing the grand opening ceremonies.
- Supplying design and space planning assistance.
- Providing the basic furniture for the SBRC.
- Assisting with technical issues in the area of telecommunications and computer technology.
- Providing initial and ongoing training for SBRC staff.
- Committing staff time to small business assistance appropriate to the size and demands of the SBRC.
- Using appropriate library-related information in publications and releases distributed to the media for promotion of the SBRC.
- Assisting in recruiting support for the various functions and activities of the library.
- Participating with the library in obtaining and displaying an up-to-date library of small business literature.
- Developing business assistance relationships with colleges and universities or other business and community groups.
- Referring appropriate clients to the SBRC for assistance.
- Supporting the library in its new and existing business assistance programs.
- Supporting and cooperating with the library on special projects and initiatives.

Commitment to the Business Center

The agreement clearly spelled out the high degree of commitment and participation by all parties in the development of the center. The library and the bank committed themselves to cooperating and sharing all kinds of resources—dollars, staff, time, expertise and equipment to make the idea of a small business resource center become a reality in the Main Library. NationsBank's role went way beyond a cash contribution to underwrite a library project. The bank was a partner in every sense of the word and as such took a keen interest in the implementation of the project. The challenge was to satisfy the different expectations of each institution.

Resolving differences

As might be expected, several issues arose during the negotiation of the agreement. The first issue that had to be resolved was the naming of the SBRC. NationsBank felt that their contribution of over $500,000 in cash and in-kind services warranted calling the center the NationsBank Small Business Resource Center. Library staff were uncomfortable with this idea. While they were accustomed to libraries and sections of libraries being named after individual benefactors, they had trouble with the idea of providing library space for the promotion of an individual business enterprise. They compared it to selling billboards in the library, and thought it threatened the neutral position of the library in the community. In addition, some felt that the cash contribution was not large enough to allow the bank to reap the benefits of this naming opportunity in perpetuity. Others felt that because NationsBank answered our request and stepped forward to fund the project that they should be given special recognition. A compromise was reached. The center was named the Broward County Library/NationsBank Small Business Resource Center to highlight the partnership concept. Use of the NationsBank name was restricted to the term of the agreement (three years) with the opportunity to negotiate an extension on the use of the name on an annual basis.

Some discussion centered around the issue of client confidentiality. NationsBank had expected to register clients in the center and use these names for follow-up mailings and to track the success of the center. This was consistent with their expectation that the center would be an intake facility for various funding programs. Library staff had real concerns about sharing this information outside of the library environment. They felt that, at the very least, clients should have to give written permission for information to be used in this way. The final draft of the contract states that "All parties' list of the names and addresses of small business concerns utilizing the SBRC shall be disclosed upon request to any cosponsor to the extent that client confidentiality is protected and the client has consented to providing such information." This compromise position provided a realistic solution that satisfied the needs of both institutions.

A budget was developed as part of the agreement that specified the contributions of each partner and showed the cash versus in-kind costs of the project. Most of the cash donated by NationsBank was earmarked for construction and start-up costs. The first year salary of the SBRC manager was also funded from the cash donation. The library director pledged to fund the position in subsequent years by adding a new position or reassigning a current position. A reserve was set aside in the second and third year of the contract to cover any unforeseen expenses. In addition to buying some new furniture for the center, the bank also committed to refurbishing furniture and equipment surplussed due to bank takeovers and consolidations. The library contributed a library specialist I to staff the center. Both institutions committed considerable staff time to program development, staff training and marketing.

It took several months to work out the differences and negotiate the final agreement between the library foundation and NationsBank. Several drafts were written and sent to the county attorney for review. It was finally signed by both parties in June 1997. A subsequent agreement between the library foundation and Broward County outlin-

Additional Funders?

From the beginning, all parties realized the need to draw other partners to the project to increase resources and involve more of the community. The library foundation and the bank both agreed to work together to recruit new partners. NationsBank, however, was insistent that no other banks be allowed to sponsor the project. This made it difficult for the library foundation to find other willing partners since so many of the foundation's corporate supporters were banks. Interest from competing banks in funding business services had to be diverted to projects other that the SBRC. Realizing the problem with recruiting partners, NationsBank reiterated its commitment to providing all of the funding necessary to get the project off the ground.

ing the responsibilities for the construction phase was signed the following month. This agreement allowed the foundation to contract for the construction and avoid some of the delays associated with the county purchasing process. By July of 1997, a major milestone had been reached, and everyone was anxious to move forward and for construction to begin.

Building a Dream

While negotiations were in progress, staff proceeded to plan and implement the reorganization of the fifth floor to accommodate the SBRC. By November of 1996, staff had cleared a 3,700 square foot area in the northwest corner of the floor, unaware that the negotiations would take much longer than the physical reorganization of the department.

The only real construction needed was to put up walls for the counseling rooms, the training room and the librarian's office and storage area. The rest of the project involved only cosmetic changes such as new carpeting and furniture. Even though it was a fairly minor construction project, it was not immune from the usual delays that haunt any construction project. Through patience, understanding, and hard work, the project was finally completed.

Figure 10.2: SBRC customers are greeted and offered assistance in using the centers many services and resources.

A New Model of Service

Upon entering the SBRC customers are greeted, offered assistance, and if new asked to register and give a brief orientation. The reference collection is geared towards existing and potential small business people. Users have access to state-of-the-art computers linked to the library's catalog, business databases, and interactive business software. Private rooms for the volunteer business counselors are available, with appointments scheduled by staff. A full schedule of training opportunities is available in the seminar room equipped with up-to-date computer and audiovisual equipment. Staff work closely with the customers, over five thousand in the first year, to determine their individual needs. This is used to tailor a program for entrepreneurial launch or expansion by developing the knowledge and skills to build a successful business.

This level of customer service requires a large corps of volunteers and partners to supplement the two full-time staff assigned to the SBRC. Under the leadership of NationsBank's vice president for community investment, representatives from the organizations and agencies who provide services to small businesses were invited to serve on an advisory committee to develop a curriculum for the SBRC. Response to this request was tremendous. All of the organizations, including the local colleges and universities, eagerly participated in this endeavor. After only a few meetings a full schedule was developed drawing on the rich resources available in the community. A number of additional partners have come on board since the opening of the center. They have conducted workshops on a wide array of topics. Operational success of the Small Business Resource Center has come through generating awareness and a commitment to service. Avenues used to reach potential users have included the library's traditional marketing, a wide distribution of SBRC literature, a website, networking with local business organizations, and all important media publicity. SBRC service quality is manifested in our focus on the center's primary users, start-up businesses, Saturday hours, and providing our own information and research intensive brand of business counseling.

Disabilities Expo

by Joann Block
Access Services Coordinator & Talking Book Librarian
Broward County Library

11

Partnership Notes
Type: Special Focus—
    Human Services
Services: Community-
    based programs
Partner since: 1979

Passage of the landmark Americans With Disabilities Act (ADA) by Congress has brought increased attention to the goal of improving access and opportunity for millions of Americans who have faced physical and psychological barriers. However, long before ADA's passage many libraries had services, programs and policies aimed at reducing barriers and increasing the public's awareness of the needs of persons with disabilities. One of the earliest programs at the national level was the National Library Service (NLS) established at the Library of Congress, which offers braille and talking books through a network of regional and subregional libraries.

Some libraries have also taken the initiative in developing partnerships with other human services organizations to improve the public's consciousness of the array of programs and services available to persons with disabilities. This chapter describes one such program, and its evolution over a period of two decades.

Introduction

The South Florida Disabilities Expo is an evolving, expanding informational, educational and social event for people with disabilities, their families and friends, caregivers and other interested individuals. Broward County Library's involvement started with the first Expo in 1979, featuring an exhibit about the Talking Book Library. As the Expo grew, Broward County Library (BCL) staff began to take a leadership role, and staff have chaired the Expo Committee for several years.

The South Florida Disabilities Expo is a true community partnership. It began as the Handicapped Expo, started by the Governor's Committee on the Employment of the Handicapped. When that organization died, the Paralyzed Veterans Association of Florida (PVAF) took on the responsibility of running the Expo. For one or two years, the Department of Vocational Rehabilitation ran the event. When they were no longer able to chair the event, the library began working closely with the PVAF to assure the Expo's continuance and success. When the ADA was approved by Congress, the Expo became the Broward Disabilities Expo, and during the last few years participation was extended to Miami-Dade and Palm Beach Counties, thus the South Florida Disabilities Expo.

The Expo is run by a committee, the composition of which has remained stable over the years. The committee includes representatives from Broward County Public Schools, Broward County Parks and Recreation, The Voice of Florida (a local rehabilitation and disability related newspaper), Paralyzed Veterans Association of Florida, United Hearing and Deaf Services, Division of Blind Services, Coral Springs Advocacy Committee for the Disabled, Florida's Department of Children and Families, Developmental Services and two representatives from BCL.

Each year, something new is added, frequently by new partners. About three years ago, the county's Office of Equal Opportunities agreed to provide funding to promote the Expo. This has allowed the Expo to buy advertising space in the local newspapers. In 1998, a local rehabilitation center, HEALTHSOUTH Sunrise

Rehabilitation Hospital, asked if they could host a "Power Hour," a reception for the Expo exhibitors and workers. This reception was designed to bring everyone together for networking and socializing before the two-day event.

For the last five years, the Expo has included a J.C. Penney Fashion Show featuring models with disabilities. For almost ten years, the Chorus of Hands has performed for the Expo. The Chorus of Hands is a volunteer troupe of sign language interpreters and exceptional education teachers who sign and dramatize songs.

Figure 11.1: Announcement for the 1998 South Florida Disabilities Expo.

For the last sixteen years, the library's exhibits were exclusively about services provided for people with disabilities. They were primarily staffed by librarians working in those departments. Two years ago, the library's Marketing Department got involved and expanded the exhibit to include all library services. This year, the library's Outreach Services has taken responsibility for planning the BCL exhibit.

The Expo is held at a shopping mall. The mall donates the space for the two-day event open during all mall hours. Attendance includes those who come specifically to see the Expo and shoppers who come upon it serendipitously. Many shoppers come away from the mall with a new awareness of disability issues and information for friends or family with disabilities. Every exhibitor has a favorite story about someone who received unexpected help because of the mall location. Other participants view the Expo as a social gathering and networking opportunity. Exhibitors and visitors congregate at the mall food court for lunch, dinner and snacks to chat and share information.

Initially, the Expo was small, and the committee borrowed tables and chairs and created their own signs. The malls required professionally made signs, so they were never told about this economy. Since everyone on the committee was a professional in his or her field, we could claim that these signs were made by professionals. It was always an inside joke that committee members could add professional signmaker to their resumes. Since the Expo has grown, a small fee is charged to exhibitors that pays a show management company to take care of the booths and signs.

The South Florida Disabilities Expo is a grass-roots project. It is a service to the community, managed by members of the community. BCL is known throughout the disability community for providing leadership and support for this event. The Expo helps make the library part of the community it is trying to serve. That is perhaps one of the best results of a community partnership.

Figure 11.2: For two days, the mall is full of people who come to socialize at the Expo, as well as those who learn from it unexpectedly.

Partnerships to Reach New Americans and the Multiethnic Community

by Tanya Simons-Oparah
Assistant Director/Outreach Services
Broward County Library

12

Partnership Notes
Type: Special Focus—
   Diversity
Services: Joint programs
   & publications
Partners since: 1993

Introduction

Many communities are experiencing major demographic changes as a result of immigration, and barring a shift in our national policies, there is every indication this trend will continue to accelerate well into the twenty-first century. The benefits of a democratic society, the nation's healthy economy, and the instability experienced in other regions of the world, are factors that are contributing to this trend. Census projections make it very clear that the ethnic composition of the U.S. will be substantially different in the twenty-first century, compared to the past. There is little doubt that this nation has been strengthened throughout its history by immigration, and our culture has been enriched because of it. Historically, the public library has played a major role in helping new Americans to cope with life in a different society and to gain citizenship. The library has also been an important resource for many individuals seeking information about their cultural heritage, and a contributor to the preservation of these varied cultures.

Over time, the type of services offered by libraries has changed. At the beginning of the twentieth century, libraries provided resources and programs designed to integrate immigrants into American society. Foreign language collections were developed, but the primary emphasis was on teaching English. At the end of the century, America is no longer the melting pot. While English is still important, the global economy requires individuals who can be fluent in a variety of languages. Libraries still have an important role in aiding immigrants to gain their citizenship and cope with our complex society, but the manner in which this is accomplished has changed. There are a variety of agencies and organizations that now exist to serve the new American, and an increasing number of entities whose express missions are to foster, preserve and celebrate these cultures in American society.

The rules have changed. It is no longer appropriate for any library to take a unilateral approach in serving the new immigrant, or to develop multiethnic collections and services without the direct involvement of the other organizations devoted to those cultures. This chapter offers several examples of how a library can partner with these organizations and agencies to better serve individuals and the community.

Background

The staff of the Broward County Library (BCL) has always thought that the library was "A Place for All Reasons." In fact, this was our marketing slogan for the opening of the Main Library in 1984. Our organizational culture could be described as "gregarious" and "out-going" because we make every effort to figuratively put our arms around everyone in our community. Nowhere is this outlook more apparent than in the programs and services the library offers to nontraditional and underserved citizens. These potential patrons range from low-income populations, with few if any information options, to the wealthiest members of the community, with a world of information choices.

Paralleling the rapid growth of Broward County since 1980 has been an equally dramatic change in the county's ethnic diversity. To meet the service requirements of these special new international populations the library developed some unique programs as the best means of marketing and making the resources of the public library known and available.

Putting aside business-as-usual and becoming involved outside of the library in community activities has been an effective approach in reaching Broward's underserved populations. Focusing on the needs of new residents and new readers and being open to ideas from community representatives of these culturally diverse populations has enabled the Outreach Services Department (OSD) staff to present the library to new audiences and gain strong community support for the library among new and emerging ethnic populations.

Originally, the OSD was involved in providing services to groups in the community that did not have ready access to the library, such as the homebound and people who resided in geographical areas without library service. The mission of the department evolved and expanded from books by mail and traveling libraries to providing services and programs for groups that are traditionally underserved library users. OSD staff actively participate in culturally specific programs and events in conjunction with community-based organizations. This approach provides an infinite number of partnering opportunities for the library.

Useful examples of projects and services that were developed through the collaboration of OSD staff with community-based organizations are the BCL/Immigration and Naturalization (INS) Partnership, *Welcome Home Newsletter*, and *Multiethnic Resource Directory*.

Library/Immigration & Naturalization Service Partnership

The Immigration and Naturalization Service (INS) in South Florida faces the challenge of serving more than 200,000 legal residents in the tri-county area of Miami/Dade, Broward and Palm Beach Counties from one office in Miami. By 1993, INS was finding it increasingly difficult to accommodate the large number of people (residents and nonresidents) who came for a wide range of services. It was able to conduct citizenship swearing-in ceremonies only once each year in Miami/Dade.

In an effort to alleviate these problems, the INS approached the library about using the Main Library's auditorium for a citizenship swearing-in ceremony. BCL was eager to have another way of serving these members of the community and to further relationships with Broward's multicultural populations. For most of the INS clients, it was the first time they had been inside a public library.

Following the first ceremony, INS realized that the Main Library offered a conveniently central location from which to conduct its business in the tri-county area, and they requested space to conduct weekly programs on how to go about renewing green cards. Each subsequent program drew substantially larger numbers of people. The average attendance during the first year was 300 to 350 per program. It quickly became apparent to the library staff that this would be a wonderful way of reaching representatives of immigrant populations. Today, these activities are held every Wednesday from 9:00 a.m. to 2:00 p.m.

From the beginning OSD staff attended the programs, distributing library information, issuing library cards, and generally making people feel welcome and comfortable. The Main Library docents soon began offering tours of the library to INS clients waiting for their appointments and later the Friends offered complimentary coupons for a continental breakfast in the library's restaurant.

The Main Library is the only public facility in Broward County where legal immigrants can renew their alien registration card, obtain naturalization and other immigration forms, meet face-to-face with an immigration officer, and receive official information about current INS procedures and requirements.

Furthermore, the library is the only site in the county where naturalization ceremonies are performed on a regular basis. BCL staff take the lead in planning the ceremonies and designing a quarterly swearing-in ceremony and program. The schedule is usually designed to coincide with other major library events, such as National Library Week in April. A welcoming reception for each group of newly naturalized citizens is hosted by the National Daughters of the American Revolution. More than 800 new citizens have been naturalized at BCL since 1993.

The quality and quantity of services offered has expanded and the number of people served has grown steadily. The large number of immigration-related questions received staff prompted the creation of a separate information response line which is available in English and Spanish. Since its inception in 1996, more than 7,000 calls have been received. The Main Library's Government Documents Department and several branches have developed a special document collection of needed information and forms to assist patrons. According to INS figures, BCL served 6,171 immigrants in 1994, 2,283 in 1995 and 4,326 in 1996.

These programs and services help BCL expand our network of affiliations within Broward County's ethnic community and market library services to the ever expanding number of new residents.

The Welcome Home Newsletter

Meeting the information needs of the county's new international, non-English-speaking population was a challenge that the library enthusiastically accepted. The OSD staff's initial effort was a newsletter published and distributed jointly with the Broward Public Schools. The *Welcome Home Newsletter* targeted the families of immigrant children in the public schools who were struggling to cope with their new surroundings, and who needed basic school, medical, transportation, and social service information. In 1996, the library responded to the school board's request for help in publishing and distributing the newsletter. The school board provided interpreters. OSD staff wrote the text. Both partners shared the costs of printing, and circulation was handled through the established distribution networks of the library and the school board. The first newsletters were published in English and Spanish. Haitian Creole language issues were added in subsequent years and a Portuguese version is in the planning stages. Today, the library has a newcomers services coordinator who is responsible for publishing and distributing the newsletter to a greatly expanded network of ethnic organizations.

This collaboration has enabled BCL to market our services to new populations and each year we refine and add materials to the library's rapidly expanding international collection. The relationships that were started and fostered with the newsletter provided the linkages that were so important in developing the county's first multiethnic resource directory.

Figure 12.1: *The Welcome Home Newsletter* was a 1996 National Association of Counties (NACO) Achievement Award winner.

Multiethnic Resource Guide

With an eye on the growth of South Florida into a cosmopolitan community, the OSD staff sought to provide an accessible, easy-to-use print directory that would complement the online information available through the Southeast Florida Library Information Network's (SEFLIN) Free-Net. Such a document would help answer patron and staff requests for information on the ethnic and multicultural development of the county.

Seeking the means for such a venture, BCL joined forces with the Broward Public Library Foundation (BPLF) and SEFLIN and sought grant funding from the Telecommunications and Information Infrastructure Assistance Program, National Telecommunications and Information Administration, and the U.S. Department of Commerce for the publication of Broward County's multiethnic resource directory.

This directory brings together in one publication the names and addresses of organizations that are involved in promoting and serving the ethnic populations in the county including civic and political groups, social clubs, community, cultural and educational organizations, festivals, governmental agencies, news media, professional networking organizations, religious organizations, sororities and fraternities, social services and health services agencies.

Because of its close working relationships with community organizations, OSD was a repository of much of the information that was to be included in the directory. The goal of the project was to compile this information and make it available to the staff and the community at large. The core database for the directory originated from the Multicultural Resource Section within SEFLIN'S Free-Net which provided information on ethnic clubs, organizations, and service providers. OSD staff felt the Free-Net database was valuable, but the information needed to be broadened.

The library foundation was a natural partner in this endeavor since it plays an active role in supporting BCL's efforts to showcase the ethnic diversity of Broward County and promote cultural understanding. As Kay Harvey, Executive Director of the Broward Public Library Foundation, stated in the introduction to the directory "we anticipate that the *Multiethnic Resource Guide* will provide not only expanded usage and greater awareness of the library's materials and services devoted to different cultures, but will provide the public with free and easy access to the many organizations that serve the varied cultures of Broward County."

Figure 12.2: The *Resource Directory* puts online community information in an accessible print format.

SEFLIN was an eager partner, since their online database could be updated and expanded at minimal cost. SEFLIN also has a strong commitment to meeting the information needs of South Florida's culturally diverse community. A printed and expanded version would reach many individuals and organizations with no access to a computer. With the conversion of SEFLIN's Free-Net to a website, it would also make the information available to the entire community—in the library and outside—through the World Wide Web.

The first directory was published in 1996 and updates are planned every two years. It was also decided that OSD would have responsibility for collecting the information and updating the directory Organizations are asked to complete a registration form, and anyone who feels their organization should be included is encouraged to submit information. Informational displays featuring a directory and registration forms are sent to all 33 BCL branches.

The *Multiethnic Resource Guide* advances the mission of all the participating organizations in a cost effective manner. The way in which this publication was developed and is maintained also illustrates the value of partnerships in serving new Americans and the multiethnic community. The participation of a variety of organization strengthens the product or service, and ensures that the library is making the best use of its own resources.

Community Technology Center

by Shirley Amore
Director
Sarasota County Libraries

13

The Community Technology Center (CTC) in the Main Library of the Broward County Library (BCL) is a good example of a technology project that grew out of an existing partnership and developed into a multifaceted program involving many organizations in the community.

Background

The CTC grew out of the Florida Diagnostic Learning Resources System (FDLRS) Media Center project, a partnership with the Broward County School District described in more detail in chapter four. In discussions between the school district's FDLRS coordinator and the director of the Main Library, it became clear that both institutions had a real need for a place to train staff on computer applications. Since the FDLRS partnership had been so successful, and the two people involved in the discussion had such a good working relationship, ideas flowed freely. The idea of developing a joint-use training center at the Main Library emerged and both parties immediately embraced the idea. After gaining support for the idea from their respective administrations, they enthusiastically began the planning process.

The first order of business was to identify an appropriate site. The Main Library was the logical choice because of its central location within the county, the availability of space in the building, and the fact that many school district services were already located in the building. The question of where to locate the training center within the building was a little more difficult to answer.

Before this question could be answered, the scope of services in the center had to be determined. Initially, the discussion focused on the original idea of a joint training center for staff. School district staff needed a place to hold computer training workshops for teachers and staff in the many computer applications used in the classroom. Library administration had long felt the need to have a place to train staff on the many functions of the computer automation system, the various electronic reference products available on the system's wide area network, and SEFLIN Free-Net. The concept grew, however, to encompass training for the public as well. Since the school district's computer environment was predominately Macintosh and the library's was MS-DOS and Windows, it was decided that two separate labs were required to meet the needs of both parties.

BCL also saw the creation of this center as an opportunity to answer a public demand for computers for personal document processing. The library had been providing typewriters for public use for some time and people began to expect that the library would keep up with technology and provide computers for word processing, spreadsheets and other personal applications.

Both school and library staff saw a need to have a place with up-to-date computer workstations to preview new multimedia computer applications. Staff had always been frustrated with their inability to preview and thoroughly test new software before purchase and felt that the general public also shared this frustration. They felt that they would be providing a great service to both staff and the public if

Partnership Notes
Type: Special Focus—
   Technology
Services: Joint facilities,
   equipment & training
Partners since: 1996

What Is the Community Technology Center?
The center opened its 5,000 square ft. facility located on the first floor of the Main Library in March 1996. There are four separate areas, each devoted to a different aspect of technology.

Computer Training Centers
There are two training labs, one running Macintosh, the other running DOS\Windows. The project started with eight Macintosh computers and thirteen IBM compatibles. It has grown to include eighteen Macintosh and twenty-eight IBM compatible computers.

Preview Center This area consists of two well-equipped stand-alone multimedia computers which allow patrons to preview new software.

Public Use Computers
This area has grown from six to twelve networked computers loaded with popular software for patrons to do word processing, spreadsheets, resumes and other personal documents.

Assistive\Adaptive Equipment for People with Disabilities This area provides a venue to display and demonstrate devices that are available to people with visual, motor and other disabilities.

they could convince major software vendors to place a free copy of new software packages in the center for preview purposes. The idea was to develop a preview collection of the latest and greatest software that patrons could test before purchase.

The library had invested a significant amount of money over the years in electronic assistive devices for people with visual impairments. These devices were housed in the FDLRS Media Center along with many samples of adaptive devices that school district technicians designed for disabled children to enhance their communication skills and learning ability. The new CTC seemed a perfect place to showcase these tools and integrate the technology services for people with disabilities with other technology-related services.

As the scope of the project grew,. the challenge was to find a space in the Main Library that was convenient for the public, accessible for the disabled and large enough to house all of these services. After some discussion, 5,000 square feet on the first floor, occupied by the FDLRS Media Center, was selected as the site for the new technology center. This glassed-walled, self-contained area on the entry level to the library provided a perfect showcase for the new technology center.

Once the site was selected, staff spent a considerable amount of time drafting a formal agreement between the school board and the county outlining the terms and responsibilities of the partnership. This is a very important step in any partnership which involves the sharing of resources because it forces the participants to be specific about their expectations of the project and of their partner. It helps ensure that everyone is on the same page and that there are no hidden agendas. This step in the process, however, requires a certain amount of patience from all concerned. In this particular case, it was a slow process involving the legal departments of two large bureaucracies and the lengthy approval process of both the county and the school board.

After several months, an agreement was finally signed. It clearly spelled out the responsibilities of each party. The wording of the agreement is included here as an illustration of the specificity needed for such an undertaking.

Figure 13.1: The agreement between the county and the school board clearly defines the responsibilities of each.

The County will provide a site for the establishment of a Technology Training and Preview Center. The Center will:
- provide a place for computer training of School Board and Library staff as well as the general public,
- allow School Board and Library staff and the public to preview software packages before purchase,
- provide computers for the general public for personal use, and
- provide a place for the display and demonstration of assistive devices for the disabled.

The County will hire, supervise and evaluate Library staff to run the Center to:
- elicit preview materials from vendors with input from partners,
- handle shipment of materials to and from vendors,
- identify software and equipment problems and alert software vendors,
- assist public in the operation of equipment and software,
- create and maintain training schedules,
- maintain software evaluation forms, and
- advise the School Board of progress/growth and development.

The School Board will:
- pay the County on a quarterly basis a total of $84,000 to fund one librarian II, one Library Associate and one Library Assistant;
- provide $58,000 for computer equipment, software and materials for the Center;
- provide information, guidance, consultation and technical assistance to the Center staff;
- provide and maintain computer hardware and furniture for the Center; and
- provide trainers and training programs to School Board personnel.

Although this document has been revised in subsequent years to clarify some issues and allow for changing needs, the agreement served well as a blueprint for building this joint-use facility, and for budgeting the operating expense.

Another key element in the success of this project was the establishment of a joint task force to implement the project. The task force which consisted of key staff from both institutions met regularly to address the many issues that arose as the project developed. As a group they tackled the complex issues of moving the FDLRS Department out of the designated area, designing the layout of the center, selecting furniture and equipment, determining staffing levels and hours of operation based on the budget, wiring and configuring computer networks and planning the dedication and opening celebration for the center. Several subcommittees worked on specific parts of the project and pulled in internal and external experts and resources as needed.

Probably the thorniest problem that the group encountered was retrofitting the room for all of the computer equipment and networks. Wiring the room to accommodate so many computers in a networked environment proved to be much more complex than was originally anticipated. Experts for the library's automation staff and the county were called in to assess the situation. They developed a plan to resolve the problems but the solution required more money and more equipment. Working as a team, staff and administration identified the needed resources and the project continued on track.

The fact that this complicated project was implemented in record time (less than a year and a half from original idea to opening day) is due in large part to the work of the task force. Members of the task force worked together in a spirit of cooperation and collaboration to resolve problems quickly and fairly. Meetings provided opportunities to share information, report on progress and brainstorm solutions to problems as they arose. Members came to the meetings with commitment to the project and a "can do" attitude. There was little room for personal or hidden agendas. This type of commitment at the staff level is critical to the success of any project but is particularly important when planning and implementing projects that involve more than one organization.

News of this idea to develop the CTC in partnership with the school board quickly reached the Main Library's other educational partners—SEFLIN; Florida Atlantic University (FAU), Florida International University (FIU) who contract for library services for their downtown Fort Lauderdale campus; and the University of South Florida (USF) and Florida State University (FSU) Library Science programs who offer classes at the Main Library. All of them had a need for computer training and were interested in taking advantage of the opportunities this center could provide their constituents.

SEFLIN is located in the Main Library, and it was the first to approach BCL with the idea of becoming a partner in the CTC. This was a logical extension of the long-standing close relationship the library has had with SEFLIN since its inception in the early 1980s.

From the beginning, the CTC was seen as a solution to the ongoing problem of providing hands-on training to staff, the public, and other users that Broward's education institutions were all facing. After some discussion between SEFLIN and the founding partners, an agreement was reached allowing SEFLIN use of the training center for SEFLIN Free-Net training and other library-related training in exchange for additional computer equipment and staff expertise. Following this model, the four previously cited education partners also agreed to provide additional equipment to the center in exchange for use of the training center.

Because of this expansion of the partnership to meet the computer training needs of several related institutions, the CTC now has a greater number of computers offering training to staff, teachers, students and the public on the library catalog, various reference databases, SEFLIN Free-Net, the Internet, as well as specialized courses like cataloging on OCLC for library science students. It is interesting to note how partnerships can continue to grow, change and flourish in an environment where open dialog and a spirit of collaboration are encouraged and fostered.

By all measurements, the CTC has been a success. All partners continue to take advantage of this facility on a monthly basis. Statistics for January of 1998, indicate that 40 classes were held in the training rooms with a total attendance of 380 people. That month, the computer training rooms were used for a wide range of training classes including Newsbank and Proquest training for library staff; training on the library's online catalog, BIGCAT, for the general public; BIGCAT training for several elementary school classes; cataloging classes for USF students; bibliographic instruction for FAU students, First Search training for FIU students, SEFLIN Free-Net classes for the public and several training sessions for teachers.

The demand on the public use computers loaded with software for word processing, spreadsheets, resumes, etc., has grown at a rapid rate. After the first year of operation, six additional computers were added, doubling the capacity of this area. Even with the increased capacity, the occupancy rate is about 60 percent and rising. In January 1998, time on the computers was scheduled by 1,364 people.

Two state-of-the-art preview workstations were added in March of 1997, and usage is averaging between 40–45 people per month. While more work could be done in this area to develop and market the preview collection, customers enjoy the convenience of being able to view software in advance of purchase.

Use of the assistive/adaptive devices area is understandably low with an average of seven people using it each month. The fact that these devices are integrated into this highly visible area, however, provides a high degree of accessibility and speaks loudly of the library's commitment to providing services to this underserved segment of the population.

So what benefits did the library derive from this partnership? The most tangible benefit is the bigger and better training facility it was able to build through cooperation and resource sharing. The facility was also completed more quickly and at a lower cost because of the collaborative effort. By developing such a high tech, state-of-the-art facility in the Main Library, BCL received a great deal of positive publicity in the community.

The library will be able to build on the trusting relationships developed during this project to take advantage of future technology enhancements. With the solid technology foundation built in the CTC, the library will explore options like distance learning with its education partners, furthering BCL's reputation and value to the community.

The CTC provided the library with many important lessons in building partnerships. The keys to success for this project were:

- trust,
- open communication,
- understanding each others needs and limitations,
- clearly stating responsibilities of each partner,
- respecting each other's position,
- planning together,
- commitment to see the project through to completion,
- celebrating the completion of the project together, and
- sharing the praise for the project and building on its success.

Figure 13.2: Patrons using the computers at the Community Technology Center.

Afterword: Something for Everyone

The Value of Partnerships to Public Libraries and Their Communities[1]

They turn people's needs into opportunity at the Broward County Library (BCL). That is what sets BCL apart, and in this editor's view, that is what made it the obvious choice for Gale Research/LJ's 1996 Library of the Year.

From the day years ago when Lowell Martin exhorted public libraries to "concentrate and strengthen," the conventional wisdom has warned that a public library must not try to provide "something for everyone," not to try to be "all things to all people." The Martin idea became the basis for the public library output measures fad. That has evolved into the current "niche marketing" movement, in which a library administrator uses the processes of the discipline of marketing to identify service targets. Those targets then become the core of the library's program.

These concepts are popular with today's breed of library directors, and many have added business school credentials to their library degrees. They proudly apply the techniques of business to the management of libraries. Public sector management in general is overburdened with marketing thinking these days.

BCL has given us another model. Director Sam Morrison and his team, like his predecessor, Cecil Beach, are quietly proving that a flexible, enterprising library can offer "something for everyone" and do it well enough to garner support from wide-ranging constituencies and build unique partnerships with a host of private businesses, public agencies, nonprofit institutions, and individuals.

Rather than assume limitations that require a library to "concentrate and strengthen," the BCL leaders have scoured the county, state, and nation for library and information needs and for partnerships with the constituencies that have those needs. The result of BCL's enterprise is a library that truly tries to provide something, if not for everyone, for a broader and deeper range of Broward County's residents than most libraries do in their jurisdictions.

The BCL model proves that whether or not a library actually provides "something for everyone," there is substantial success in giving it a try. At BCL they continuously strive to be all library things to all people. From where I sit, that is clearly a better model than niche marketing for a tax-supported library serving a population that is as economically, ethnically, politically, and socially diverse as that of Broward County. BCL really had no choice but to turn the immense information and library needs of Broward County's hugely varied population into opportunities.

The result is an incredible 500 partnerships with all kinds of private and public agencies, including government jurisdictions. The result is a 33-unit library system well stocked with current technology and all connected in local, regional, and national networks created with new partners. The result is a public library that provides full-scale academic and research library services and resources to the students, staff, and faculties of a university, a community college, and public schools. The result is a public library with a rare book and historically document collection of note, a technology center, a business resource center for small firms, a thriving children's service, and a host of specialized services, all based on specific partnerships with the constituency in need.

The BCL lessons are clear: You can come close to meeting all the needs of the community if you are willing to risk shared control. You can do it if you don't mind taking on the toughest kinds of partnerships across turf boundaries, political jurisdictions, and agency boards. You can do it if you're energetic enough to constantly scour the jurisdiction to find new needs to meet.

In short, you can build a library system that will serve the information and education needs of all the people, and you can double the support of that system with the help of your partners. In that scenario, the measure of success is not circulation or other output measures. Success in Broward County is measured in the variety and number of library and information needs fulfilled. It is the difference between counting loans at the circulation desk and counting the winning votes at budget time.

Notes
1. John N. Berry. "Editorial: Something for Everyone." *Library Journal* (June 15, 1996) p. 6. Reprinted with permission of the author from *Library Journal*, Copyright © 1996, Cahners Business Information.

JOHN N. BERRY III
Editor-in-Chief, *Library Journal*

Resources On the Highsmith Press Website

Partnership Agreements

The following agreements were discussed in this handbook, and are provided to illustrate the terms and conditions that were agreed upon by the cooperating parties. Because legal requirements vary in many states and local jurisdictions, it is recommended that libraries wishing to enter into cooperative agreements with other public and private entities consult with their institution's legal counsel. Agreements 1 and 2 can be found both at the website and in the two appendices that follow. Additional contracts for the operation of the Small Business Resource Center and the joint-use facility with the Broward Community College can be located only by accessing the ⁣**Links** http://www.hpress.highsmith.com/lynap.htm

1. Agreement between **Broward County and Florida Atlantic University** for joint use of the facilities and services of Main Library of the Broward County Division of Libraries.

2. Agreement between **Broward County and the Broward County School Board** to provide for cooperative services between the Broward County Division of Libraries and the School Board, including the Florida Diagnostic and Learning Resource System.

3. Agreement between **Broward County and the Broward Public Library Foundation** for the operation of a small business resource center, in cooperation with **NationsBank**.

4. Agreement between **Broward County and the Broward Community College** for the joint use of the facilities and services of the North Regional Library of the Broward County Division of Libraries.

Appendix A

Agreement
Between
BROWARD COUNTY
and
FLORIDA ATLANTIC UNIVERSITY

This is an Agreement entered into on the date last appearing below by and between: BROWARD COUNTY, a political subdivision of the State of Florida, its successors and assigns, hereinafter referred to as "COUNTY," through its Board of County Commissioners.

AND

FLORIDA ATLANTIC UNIVERSITY, acting for and on behalf of the Board of Regents, a public corporation of the State of Florida, hereinafter referred to as "FAU."

WHEREAS, this Agreement is for the purpose of defining the terms and conditions under which the Broward County Public Library System's Main Library ("BCPLS") will utilize Four Hundred and Sixty Eight Thousand, Eight Hundred and Forty Five Dollars ($468,845) provided for library resources to be included in the inventories of FAU and Florida International University ("FIU") and for library services.

NOW, THEREFORE, the parties hereto have agreed on the terms and conditions governing the use of Four Hundred and Sixty Eight Thousand, Eight Hundred and Forty Five Dollars ($468,845).

1. It is agreed that the Four Hundred and Sixty Eight Thousand, Eight Hundred and Forty Five Dollars ($468,845) is for the acquisition of library resources (books, nonprint materials, serials, equipment) for maintenance, personnel and services and network services in support of the curriculum and academic programs provided by FAU and FIU in Broward County.

2. It is agreed that the library materials (books, nonprint materials, serials, and equipment) purchased from the Four Hundred and Sixty Eight, Eight Hundred and Forty Five Dollars ($468,845) provided for with these funds will be included in the total library materials inventories for FAU and FIU as determined by FAU.

3. FAU will determine the amount of these funds which will be spent for the benefit and inventory of each institution. FAU will forward funds in the amount of Four Hundred and Sixty Eight Thousand, Eight Hundred and Forty Five Dollars ($468,845) to BCPLS for the purchase of library resources (books, nonprint materials, serials, equipment) and for maintenance, personnel and library services for itself and for FIU, pursuant to conditions specified below.

4. Subsequent to the release of such funds to BCPLS for purchase of all library materials intended for the FAU and FIU inventories, BCPLS will retain detailed inventory information on such materials and make them available to the other parties as desired.

5. BCPLS shall provide the same general library services and hours of operation for FAU/FIU and their students, faculty and staff that it provides for its regular clientele except that it may also provide other academic library services and hours needed by the Universities, and shall specifically provide the following:
    a) Ordering and cataloging of materials requested by FAU and FIU, including possible provision to FAU of an OCLC/MARC compatible tape record of its holdings from 1985/86 to date for inclusion into its LUIS database.
    b) Processing, shelving, and maintenance of all resource materials selected or submitted by FAU/FIU in accordance with this Agreement.
    c) Reserve book operation, including the production and maintenance of a reserve book list.

      d) Reference assistance.

      e) Interlibrary loan services to FAU/FIU students and faculty, with provision that first access point is FAU or FIU through use of the SEFLIN compact.

      f) Circulation of library materials without numerical limitation, including granting of semester borrowing privileges to FAU and FIU faculty teaching courses and, upon recommendation of a major advisor, to Graduate Students enrolled in courses in Broward County.

      g) Bibliographic orientation for individuals and for classes.

      h) Audio visual services (on BCPLS premises only), and provision of audio visual materials, including films, tape, discs, software and other forms of audio-visual media, purchased with these funds for use in the Broward Tower. Within copyright guidelines BCPL will participate in AV exchanges with FAU and FIU.

      i) Maintenance of equipment purchased this year and in previous years in support of all contract services.

6.   The primary purpose of this Agreement is to secure library materials and associated equipment and services necessary to support FAU/FIU academic programs at the Broward Tower. FAU represents to COUNTY that it is duly authorized to make any and all representations under this Agreement concerning the rights, duties and obligations of Florida International University (FIU). Expenditures of the $468,845 shall be directly related to support of such programs. Unexpended portions of these funds originally earmarked for equipment and services will be applied to the purchase of library materials.

7.   BCPLS shall provide current and cumulative statistical data as required by the Board of Regents. BCPLS shall also submit monthly expense reports for all expenditure of funds in a timely fashion, including reports of individual titles ordered and individual pieces of equipment ordered, for the inventory reporting needs of FAU and FIU as defined by the Board of Regents Budget Office. Such statistical data and monthly annual reports shall be sent to:

BCPLS shall also furnish the above-named individuals with copies of annual financial reports covering the contract year, when distributed.

8.   Release of funds shall be made by FAU to BCPLS quarterly, $117,211.25, due on the last date of each quarter contingent upon receipt of monthly and statistical reports, as detailed in Section 7 above. Equipment purchased in previous contract years will be inventoried by BCPLS and by FAU.

9.   FAU and FIU shall select the library materials which comprise their respective inventories and shall either forward specific item requests to BCPLS or specify subject areas for approval plan purchase by BCPLS. However, BCPLS has the right not to accept any FAU/FIU library materials for custody and/or circulation which its governing authority may reject. Any such items will be returned to FAU or FIU. The books and other materials purchased on behalf of FAU and FIU are the property of FAU and FIU and shall be so indicated in or on each physical unit. This is not intended in any way to preclude or prevent BCPLS from processing or handling these materials according to its current procedures.

10.   Items in the inventory purchased with these funds are intended for use by FAU/FIU students and faculty at the Broward Tower, as well as for use by the general citizenry. Such items will be located at the main downtown location of the BCPLS and will not be withdrawn or transferred elsewhere, in whole or in part, without the consent of FAU.

11.   In the event of discontinuance of funding by the Florida Legislature in subsequent years, or the termination of this contract, all materials and equipment comprising the inventories which have been purchased with funds in this year and Special Appropriation funds in previous contract years shall revert to the respective universities unless otherwise provided for in a subsequent agreement.

12.   The books and other items in the inventory will be processed, maintained, circulated, or otherwise made available in the same manner as like materials belonging to BCPLS. FAU and FIU will not hold BCPLS liable for books lost or damaged in the course of normal use. However, when applicable, BCPLS will attempt to recover any loss or damage incurred by patrons to items in the inventory in accordance with its policies and procedures as they apply to like materials in its collections. BCPLS will notify FAU and FIU regarding any lost or damaged materials, so as to enable removal from inventory.

13. In addition to money applied to purchasing of book and nonprint materials for FAU and FIU inventories, a sum of such money may be spent for services from the Southeast Florida Library Information Network (SEFLIN), an incorporated nonprofit network based at BCPLS which facilitates the sharing of resources among libraries and their users in South Florida.

14. All FAU and FIU students and employees, with proper identification, shall be treated as Broward County residents with reference to having access to the books, equipment, and services provided by the BCPLS.

15. The term of this Agreement shall commence on July 1, 1998 and extend through June 30, 1999. The parties hereto acknowledge that these funds are for the year 1998/99 and may not recur without further legislative appropriation. This contract may be amended, terminated, or superseded by mutual agreement of the two parties or by either party on 90-day advance written notice. In the event of termination by the mutual agreement of the parties or by either party, BCPLS shall be paid for all outstanding invoices or obligations incurred prior to the date of termination. Further no modification, amendment or alteration in the terms or conditions contained herein shall be effective unless contained in a written document prepared with the same or similar formality as this Agreement and executed by FAU and by the Board of County Commissioners.

16. BCPLS will be compensated for provision of each service or purchase of materials and equipment (as specified in Section 5 above) according to schedule of payment, as listed in Exhibit A attached, with the proviso noted in section 8 above.

17. If reimbursement for any travel expenses is sought, such reimbursement must comply with Sections 287.058(1)(b) and 112.061, Florida Statutes.

18. County shall allow public access to all documents, papers, letters or other materials subject to the provisions of Chapter 119, Florida Statutes, and made or received by the County in conjunction with this Agreement. Refusal by the County to allow such public access shall be grounds for cancellation of this Agreement by FAU.

19. a. Pursuant to Section 215.422(3)(b), Florida Statutes, a state agency is required to mail a requested payment within forty (40) days after receipt of an acceptable invoice and receipt, and after inspection and acceptance of the goods, services or both, if provided in accordance with the terms and conditions of the Agreement. Failure to mail the warrant within 40 days shall result in the agency paying interest at a rate of one percent per month on the unpaid balance. The interest penalty shall be mailed within 15 days after mailing the warrant. If a party has any question regarding payment under an invoice, the party may contact the Ombudsman for the State of Florida at telephone numbers 904-488-2924 or 1-800-848-3792.

    b. Bills and invoices for fees or other compensation for services or expenses shall cite the Agreement number and shall be submitted to the Controller in detail sufficient for a proper preaudit and postaudit of them. Each bill or invoice must clearly identify the services, portion of services and expenses for which compensation is sought. Payment will be tendered only for services completed prior to the submission of the bill or invoice, or for expenses incurred prior to such submission, or both.

20. Each party assumes any and all risk of personal injury, death and property damage attributable to the willful or negligent acts or omissions of that party and its officers, employees and agents.

21. The validity, construction and effect of this Agreement shall be governed by the laws of the State of Florida. Venue for litigation concerning this Agreement shall be in Broward County, Florida. FAU and County are each entitled to the benefits of sovereign immunity, including immunities from taxation. In the event either party is required to obtain from any governmental authority any permit, license or authorization as a prerequisite to perform its obligations under this Agreement, the cost shall be borne by the party required to obtain such permit, license or authorization.

22. FAU shall not unlawfully discriminate against any person in its operations or activities under this Agreement and shall affirmatively comply with applicable provisions of the Americans with Disabilities Act (ADA) in the course of providing any services funded in whole or in part by COUNTY, including Titles I and II of the ADA (regarding non discrimination on the basis of disability, and all applicable regulations, guidelines and standards).

23. FAU decisions regarding the delivery of services under this Agreement shall be made without regard to or consideration of race, age, religion, color, gender, sexual orientation (Broward County Code Chapter 16 1/2), national origin, marital status, physical or mental disability, political affiliation or any other factor which cannot be lawfully or appropriately used as basis for service delivery

24. FAU shall comply with Title I of the Americans with Disabilities Act, regarding nondiscrimination on the basis of disability in employment and further shall not discriminate against any employee or applicant for employment because of race, age, religion, color, gender, sexual orientation (Broward County Code Chapter 16 1/2), national origin, political affiliation or physical or mental disability. In addition FAU shall take affirmative steps to ensure nondiscrimination in employment against disabled persons. Such actions shall include, but not be limited to, the following: employment, upgrading, demotion, transfer, recruitment or recruitment advertising, layoff, termination, rates of pay, other forms of compensation, terms and conditions of employment, training (including apprenticeship) and accessibility.

25. FAU shall take affirmative action to ensure that applicants are employed and employees are treated with regard to race, age, religion, color, gender, sexual orientation (Broward County Code, Chapter 16 1/2), national origin, marital status, political affiliation or physical or mental disability during employment. Such actions shall include, but not be limited to the following: employment, upgrading, demotion, transfer, recruitment or recruitment advertising, layoffs, termination or rates of pay.

26. FAU shall not engage in or commit any discriminatory practice in violation of the Broward County Human Rights Act (Broward County Code 16 1/2) in performing the Scope of Services or any part of the scope of services of this Agreement.

27. The performance of the University's obligations under this Agreement shall be subject to and contingent upon the availability of funds appropriated by the Legislature or otherwise lawfully expendable for the purpose of this Agreement for the current and future periods. The University shall give notice to Vendor of the non-availability of such funds when University has knowledge. Upon receipt of such notice by Vendor, Vendor shall be entitled to payment only for those services performed prior to the date notice was received.

28. In accordance with the Public Entity Crimes Act (Section 287.133, Florida Statutes) a person or affiliate who has been placed on the convicted vendor list maintained by the State of Florida Department of Management Services following a conviction for a public entity crime may not submit a bid on a contract, may not be awarded or perform work as a Consultant, supplies or subcontractor and may not conduct business with the University for a period of thirty six (36) months from the date of being placed on the convicted vendor list. Violation of this section by Vendor shall result in termination of this Agreement and may cause debarment.

29. This document contains the entire understanding and agreement of the parties. This document incorporates and includes all prior negotiations, correspondence, conversations, agreements and understandings applicable to the matters contained herein and the parties agree that there are no commitments, agreements or understandings concerning the subject matter of this Agreement that are not contained in this document. Accordingly the parties agree that no deviation from the terms hereof shall be predicated upon any prior representations or agreements, whether oral or written. It is further agreed that no modification, amendment or alteration in the terms or conditions contained shall be effective unless contained in a written document executed by FAU and the Board for the COUNTY.

30. Neither FAU nor its employees shall have or hold any continuing or frequently recurring employment or contractual relationship that is substantially antagonistic or incompatible with FAU's loyal and conscientious exercise of judgment related to its performance under this Agreement.

     IN WITNESS WHEREOF, the parties hereto have made and executed this Agreement on the respective dates under each signature: **BROWARD COUNTY** through its **BOARD OF COUNTY COMMISSIONERS**, signing by and through its Chairman, authorized to execute same by Board action, and **FLORIDA ATLANTIC UNIVERSITY**, for and on behalf of the Florida Board of Regents, signing by and through its President, duly authorized to execute same.

Appendix B

Master Agreement
Between
BROWARD COUNTY
and
THE SCHOOL BOARD OF BROWARD COUNTY, FLORIDA
for
INTERLOCAL COOPERATIVE PARTNERSHIP SERVICES FOR
FISCAL YEAR 1998 - 1999

This is an Agreement, made and entered into by and between: **BROWARD COUNTY**, a political subdivision of the state of Florida, hereinafter referred to as "**COUNTY**,"

AND

THE SCHOOL BOARD OF BROWARD COUNTY, FLORIDA, hereinafter referred to as "**SCHOOL BOARD**."

WHEREAS, COUNTY and SCHOOL BOARD actively support and endorse the concept of working together to provide services to students, parents, educators, and the Broward County community; and

WHEREAS, COUNTY and SCHOOL BOARD desire to enter into this Agreement to provide for interlocal cooperative partnership services for fiscal year 1998 to 1999; NOW THEREFORE,

IN CONSIDERATION of the mutual terms, conditions, promises, covenants and payments hereinafter set forth, the COUNTY and the SCHOOL BOARD agree as follows:

ARTICLE 1

DEFINITIONS AND IDENTIFICATIONS

1.1   **Agreement** – means this document, Articles 1 through 9, inclusive. Other terms and conditions are included in the exhibits and documents that are expressly incorporated by reference.

1.2   **Board** – The Broward County Board of County Commissioners.

1.3   **Contract Administrator** – The Broward County Administrator, the Director of the Broward County Libraries Division, or the designee of such County Administrator or Director. The primary responsibilities of the Contract Administrator are to coordinate and communicate with SCHOOL BOARD and to manage and supervise execution and completion of the Scope of Services and the terms and conditions of this Agreement as set forth herein. In the administration of this Agreement, as contrasted with matters of policy, all parties may rely on the instructions or determinations made by the Contract Administrator; provided, however, that such instructions and determinations do not change the Scope of Services.

1.4   **County Attorney** – The chief legal counsel for COUNTY who directs and supervises the Office of the County Attorney pursuant to Section 4.03 of the Broward County Charter.

1.5   **Project** – The Project consists of the services described in Article 2.

ARTICLE 2

SCOPE OF SERVICES

2.1   COUNTY and SCHOOL BOARD shall perform all work identified in Article 2 herein in this Agreement. The parties agree that the scope of services is a description of the parties' obligations and responsibilities and is deemed to include preliminary considerations and prerequisites, and all labor, materials, equipment, and tasks which are such an inseparable part of the work described that exclusion would render performance impractical, illogical, or unconscionable.

2.2   COUNTY and SCHOOL BOARD acknowledge and agree that the Contract Administrator has no authority to make changes that would increase, decrease, or otherwise modify the Scope of Services to be provided under this Agreement.

2.3   COUNTY and SCHOOL BOARD agree that both parties shall jointly and cooperatively administer and operate the following programs:

2.3.1 The Professional Collection located at the COUNTY's Main Library and integrated into the library's collection. The collection includes educational materials in multiple formats.

2.3.2 Participating schools/library media centers which are operated during the summer school sessions. This program is designed to improve library services for young persons and families in various neighborhoods which do not have public library facilities within the neighboring community. Funding for staff shall be provided by the COUNTY. Management of program and staff shall be the responsibility of the SCHOOL BOARD.

2.3.3 The COUNTY's Annual Children's Reading Festival which brings authors, illustrators, and storytellers to the COUNTY's Main Library. The School Board's support shall include providing information to the schools' students and staff, soliciting volunteers to help with the Festival and staffing a Reading Across Broward booth.

2.3.4 The Reading Across Broward Program which is a reading motivation program designed to motivate children to become lifelong readers and users of the library. As a Partner in Excellence, the Broward County Library purchases and provides books listed on Reading Across Broward bibliographies; supports the annual Read In, Career Days, Summer Reading Program, and other activities; offers public library card applications through schools; and offers interlibrary loan between the public libraries and the schools. The SCHOOL BOARD provides bibliographies for use in the public libraries. Both COUNTY and SCHOOL BOARD shall serve on the Reading Across Broward Steering Committee.

2.3.5 The Florida Diagnostic and Learning Resource Systems (FDLRS) Media Center located at the COUNTY's Main Library which provides teachers, parents, care givers of exceptional students, and university students involved in exceptional student education greater access to learning resources. The collection consists of educational materials in multiple formats.

2.3.6 The Florida Diagnostic and Learning Resources Systems (FDLRS) Regional Assistive Technology Education Network ("Access Preview Center") and the Florida Alliance for Assistive Services and Technology (FAAST) program at the COUNTY's Main Library which serves teachers, parents, care givers of exceptional students, and university students involved in exceptional student education in Region 5. Operation of the Access Preview Center and provision of services shall be the joint responsibility of COUNTY and SCHOOL BOARD.

2.3.7 The Family Network on Disabilities at the COUNTY's Main Library which provides specialized services for parents of children with disabilities and students at risk. These services are provided by parents who are volunteering for the SCHOOL BOARD. SCHOOL BOARD shall be responsible for operation of the Family Network on Disabilities, providing furnishings and materials, and shall be responsible and liable for the children, the parents and the volunteers using or providing the specialized services of the Family Network on Disabilities.

2.3.8 The Broward Community Technology Center which is located at the COUNTY's Main Library.

2.3.9 The Adult English for Speakers of Other Languages ("ESOL") International Festival which promotes Adult ESOL programs and increases multi-cultural sensitivity in the community. This festival is held annually at the Broward County Main Library. COUNTY shall provide the site and technical support for the event.

2.3.10 The Broward County Literacy Coalition jointly supported by both COUNTY and SCHOOL BOARD through the Department of Vocational, Adult and Community Education. The Literacy Coalition facilitates sharing of information and services among groups involved in the field of adult literacy. The Literacy Coalition also heightens public awareness of the problem of low literacy among members of the Broward County community. COUNTY and SCHOOL BOARD shall jointly provide staff and clerical support for this program.

2.3.11 SCHOOL BOARD shall provide one of its employees to serve as the Adult and Community Education Volunteer Liaison. COUNTY shall provide office space and a telephone, including voice mail, for use by the Liaison. The Liaison and the COUNTY Read Campaign representative shall work collaboratively with recruitment efforts to recruit volunteer tutors and to recruit adult students with limited literacy skills.

2.3.12   Training of literacy tutors by the COUNTY for the Read Campaign and for Literacy Volunteers of America (LVA).

2.3.13   Coordination of literacy classes to include Adult English for Speakers of other Languages (ESOL), General Educational Development (GED) or Adult Basic Education (ABE), or other offerings between COUNTY and SCHOOL BOARD which will avoid unwarranted duplication. COUNTY and SCHOOL BOARD agree that space shall be provided at the most appropriate site with the prior consent of the site provider when such space is available.

2.3.14   Homework Assistance Centers. Through joint cooperative arrangements, SCHOOL BOARD shall provide coordination and staffing for the programs and the Library will provide the space for the program when such space is available.

2.3.15   Mail services between the schools and the COUNTY's public libraries which shall be expedited by pick up and delivery services to the Main Library operated by SCHOOL BOARD's delivery/mail service.

2.3.16   Display of school projects and performance opportunities for magnet schools' Performing Arts activities at the COUNTY's libraries. Such programs enhance outreach efforts into the community and help the public become more knowledgeable about various schools' activities.

2.3.17   Provide each other with facilities for meeting and training purposes when space is available at the provider's site with the prior consent of such site provider.

2.4   COUNTY does promise and agree to provide services for SCHOOL BOARD's Professional Collection (hereinafter referred to as "Professional Collection") as follows:

2.4.1   Operation of the Professional Collection.

2.4.2   Maintain the Professional Collection database and create annotated bibliographies of recent additions to the collection on a quarterly basis.

2.4.3   Provide statistical reports to Learning Resources regarding usage including searches, faxes, phone responses, pony delivery, and other related usage and services delivered on a monthly basis.

2.4.4   Hire, supervise, and evaluate library staff to operate the Professional Collection who shall provide services as follows:
    a.   reference materials and assistance in their use.
    b.   information and referral to other resource agencies.
    c.   library books and other circulating materials which are delivered by request through SCHOOL BOARD's pony and the Library's delivery system.
    d.   periodicals, serials, and selected ephemeral materials.
    e.   audiovisual materials and other materials as jointly deemed appropriate.
    f.   bibliographies as requested.

2.4.5   Supervise the Professional Collection staff and provide services necessary to operate the collection on a daily basis.

2.4.6   Provide space to accommodate the Professional Collection's furnishings and collections in the COUNTY's Main Library.

2.5   COUNTY does promise and agree to provide the following services for the administration and operation of the Florida Diagnostic and Learning Resource System (Media Center) as follows:

2.5.1   Operate the Florida Diagnostic and Learning Resources System (hereinafter referred to as "FDLRS") Media Center.

2.5.2   Systematically document and track the circulation of all materials in the FDLRS/HRD collection until collection is added to the County Library database.

2.5.3   Provide data reports as requested by the FDLRS Coordinator.

2.5.4   Hire, supervise, and evaluate library staff to run the FDLRS Media Center to provide the following:
    a.   reference materials and assistance in their use.
    b.   information and referral to other resource agencies.

    c.   library books and other circulating materials which are delivered by request through SCHOOL BOARD's pony and the Library's delivery system.

    d.   periodicals, serials, and selected ephemeral materials.

    e.   audiovisual materials and other materials jointly deemed appropriate.

    f.   bibliographies as requested.

2.5.5   Supervise the FDLRS Media Center's staff and provide services necessary to operate the Media Center on a daily basis.

2.5.6 Provide adequate space to accommodate the furnishings and the collections of FDLRS Media Center and the Family Network on Disabilities. The parties agree that any special furnishings or collections necessary to support the Family Network on Disabilities shall be provided by SCHOOL BOARD.

2.5.7   Provide parents of ESE (Exceptional Student Education) students the ability to return and obtain FDLRS media materials at all Broward County Library branches.

2.5.8   Provide space at Main Library to accommodate the following:

    a.   approximately fifty (50) boxes containing Add-On Certification in service materials (Boxes are a white cardboard 16"x12"x10" with lids.)

    b.   access for SCHOOL BOARD's interschool main delivery service (Pony) vehicle.

2.6   COUNTY does promise and agree to provide the following services for the administration and operation of the Broward Community Technology Center.

2.6.1   COUNTY does promise and agree to provide a site, for the establishment of the Broward Community Technology Center and to provide services as follows:

    a.   a place for computer training for staffs of SCHOOL BOARD and the COUNTY's Library as well as the general public;

    b.   allow SCHOOL BOARD and COUNTY's library staff and the public to preview software packages before purchase;

    c.   computers for the general public to use; and

    d.   space for the display and demonstration of assistive devices for disabled users.

2.6.2   COUNTY does promise and agree to hire, supervise and evaluate library staff to operate and administer the Broward Community Technology Center, and to provide services as follows:

    a.   elicit preview materials from vendors with input from any partner(s) and SCHOOL BOARD.

    b.   handle shipment of materials to and from vendors.

    c.   identify software and equipment problems and alert software vendors.

    d.   assist the general public in the operation of equipment and software.

    e.   create and maintain training schedules.

    f.   maintain software evaluation forms.

    g.   advise SCHOOL BOARD of progress/growth and development.

2.7   SCHOOL BOARD does promise and agree to provide the following services for the administration and operation of the Broward Community Technology Center:

    a.   trainers and training programs for school board personnel.

    b.   in-kind goods and services in the approximate amount of Fifty-eight Thousand Dollars ($58,000.00) for the purchase and maintenance of computer equipment, software, furnishings, and materials for the Broward Community Technology Center.

2.8   SCHOOL BOARD and COUNTY shall continue to seek additional cooperative partnership activities and to expand those listed in this Agreement. The parties' immediate efforts shall focus on sharing existing resources and connecting all Broward County schools and Broward County public libraries in order to increase access to community resources. The parties' immediate activities shall include:

2.8.1   Participation in SEFLIN Free-Net, an electronic database of community information and BigCat, the Broward County Library's computerized information system. SCHOOL BOARD shall participate in SEFLIN Free-Net as both an information user, with students, staff and administration having access to these resources, and as an information provider, responsible for providing and updating the data available through the Education Menu.

2.8.2 Determining technological solutions in order to provide equitable access to SEFLIN Free-Net and BigCat for schools and administrative units.

2.8.3 Providing awareness training and application in the use of BigCat and SEFLIN Free-Net. The parties shall explore the feasibility of awarding in service points.

2.8.4 Providing of instructional television linkage at the Main Library.

2.8.5. Identifying grant sources for combined school and public library activities.

ARTICLE 3

TERM AND TIME OF PERFORMANCE

3.1 The term of this Agreement shall commence on October 1, 1998, and shall extend through September 30, 1999, with an option to renew on a yearly basis. COUNTY or SCHOOL BOARD may give notice of its intention not to renew the agreement by giving the other party forty-five (45) working days written notice of its intention not to renew prior to the last day of the term of this Agreement.

3.2 If this agreement is not renewed or a new contract is not developed between COUNTY and SCHOOL BOARD, COUNTY shall return to SCHOOL BOARD all books, periodicals, equipment, and any other materials of the Professional Collection and FDLRS Media Center as well as equipment in the Broward Community Technology Center purchased specifically for use by SCHOOL BOARD.

3.3 All duties, obligations, and responsibilities of COUNTY and SCHOOL BOARD required by this Agreement shall be completed no later than the last day of the term of this Agreement. Time shall be deemed to be of the essence in performing the duties, obligations and responsibilities required by this Agreement.

3.4 This Agreement may be terminated for convenience by SCHOOL BOARD or by COUNTY, upon action of its Board or its County Administrator, upon thirty (30) days written notice by the terminating party's Contract Administrator to the other party. Both parties acknowledge that ten dollars ($10.00) of the compensation to be paid by the other party, receipt of which is hereby acknowledged by the other party, is given as specific consideration to the other party of the right to terminate for convenience.

ARTICLE 4

COMPENSATION, METHOD OF BILLING AND PAYMENT

4.1 The SCHOOL BOARD shall be responsible for paying COUNTY the total amount of Two Hundred Forty-eight Thousand Two Hundred Dollars and Thirty-eight Cents ($248,200.38) pursuant to this Agreement. SCHOOL BOARD shall be responsible for paying COUNTY the sum of Forty-Two Thousand Two Hundred Dollars and Thirty-eight Cents ($42,200.38) for the Professional Collection ($32,200.38 salary and benefits plus $10,000 for materials); One Hundred Fourteen Thousand Dollars ($114,000.00) for the FDLRS Media Center; and Ninety-two Thousand Dollars ($92,000.00) for the Community Technology Center.

4.1.1 COUNTY shall invoice SCHOOL BOARD quarterly for the sum of Thirty-two Thousand Two Hundred Dollars and Thirty-eight Cents ($32,200.38) payable on a quarterly basis in three installment payments of Eight Thousand Fifty Dollars and Ten Cents ($8,050.10), with a fourth and final installment payment of Eight Thousand Fifty Dollars and Eight Cents ($8,050.08), for the employment by COUNTY of one Library Specialist I to operate the Professional Collection. The quarterly invoice for the Library Specialist I–Professional Collection should be sent to the Director of Learning Resources for SCHOOL BOARD within thirty (30) days of the commencement of each quarterly period and shall be payable by SCHOOL BOARD within thirty (30) days of submission of a quarterly invoice by COUNTY.

4.1.2 COUNTY shall invoice SCHOOL BOARD annually for the sum of Ten Thousand Dollars ($10,000.00) payable for the purchase of print and non-print materials for the Professional Collection. The annual invoice shall be sent to the Director of Learning Resources within thirty (30) days of the commencement of the Agreement for each annual period and shall be payable by SCHOOL BOARD within thirty (30) days of submission of an annual invoice by COUNTY.

4.1.3 COUNTY shall invoice SCHOOL BOARD quarterly for a total sum of One Hundred Fourteen Thousand Dollars ($114,000.00) which shall be payable in quarterly installments of Twenty-eight Thousand Five

Hundred Dollars ($28,500.00) for providing space and staff consisting of one Library Specialist I, one Library Specialist III and one Library Assistant for the Florida Diagnostic and Learning Resource System ("FDLRS") Media Center. The quarterly invoice for FDLRS shall be sent by COUNTY to the FDLRS Coordinator for SCHOOL BOARD within thirty (30) days of the commencement of each quarterly period and shall be payable by SCHOOL BOARD within thirty (30) days of submission of a quarterly invoice by COUNTY.

4.1.4   COUNTY shall invoice SCHOOL BOARD quarterly for the Broward Community Technology Center for a total sum of Ninety-two Thousand Dollars ($92,000.00) for the employment of one Librarian II, one Library Specialist I, and one Library Assistant which shall be payable in quarterly installments of Twenty-three Thousand Dollars ($23,000.00) by SCHOOL BOARD within thirty (30) days of submission of a quarterly invoice by COUNTY to SCHOOL BOARD.

4.2   It is acknowledged and agreed by COUNTY that the total amount of $248,200.38 is the maximum amount payable and constitutes a limitation upon SCHOOL BOARD's obligation to compensate COUNTY for its services to under this Agreement.

4.3   METHOD OF BILLING AND PAYMENT

4.3.1   COUNTY shall submit invoices to SCHOOL BOARD for payment on a quarterly basis as provided in subsections 4.1.1, 4.1.3, and 4.1.4, above within thirty (30) days of the commencement of each quarterly period.

4.3.2   COUNTY shall submit invoices for payment on an annual basis as provided in subsection 4.1.2 above within thirty (30) days of the commencement of the term of the Agreement.

4.3.3   Invoices shall designate the nature of the services to be performed, a description of the item for which the invoices are being submitted, and the expenses incurred, if any.

4.3.4   SCHOOL BOARD shall pay COUNTY within thirty (30) calendar days of date of submission of COUNTY's invoice statement.

4.4   Notwithstanding any provision of this Agreement to the contrary, either party may withhold, in whole or in part, payment to the extent necessary to protect itself from loss on account of inadequate or defective work which has not been remedied or from loss due to fraud or reasonable evidence indicating fraud by the other party. When the above reasons for withholding payment are removed or resolved in a manner satisfactory to Contract Administrator, payment may be made. The amount withheld shall not be subject to payment of interest by the party who withholds said payments.

4.5   Payment shall be made payable to "Broward County" and sent to COUNTY at the name and address below:

ARTICLE 5

CHANGES IN SCOPE OF SERVICES

5.1   Any change to the Scope of Services must be accomplished by a written amendment, executed by the parties in accordance with Section 9.18 below.

ARTICLE 6

INDEMNIFICATION

6.1   SCHOOL BOARD is a state agency as defined in Section 768.28, Florida Statutes, and agrees to be fully responsible for acts and omissions of its agents or employees to the extent permitted by law. Nothing herein is intended to serve as a waiver of sovereign immunity by any party to which sovereign immunity may be applicable. Nothing herein shall be construed as consent by a state agency or political subdivision of the State of Florida to be sued by third parties in any matter arising out of this Agreement.

6.2   COUNTY is a state agency as defined in Section 768.28, Florida Statutes, and agrees to be fully responsible for acts and omissions of its agents or employees to the extent permitted by law. Nothing herein is intended to serve as a waiver of sovereign immunity by any party to which sovereign immunity may be applicable. Nothing herein shall be construed as consent by a state agency or political subdivision of the State of Florida to be sued by third parties in any matter arising out of this Agreement.

ARTICLE 7

INSURANCE, SOVEREIGN IMMUNITY AND LIABILITY

7.1   SCHOOL BOARD is a state agency as defined by Section 768.28, Florida Statutes. SCHOOL BOARD shall furnish COUNTY's Contract Administrator with written verification of liability protection in accordance with state law prior to final execution of said Agreement.

7.2   COUNTY is a state agency as defined by Section 768.28, Florida Statutes. COUNTY shall furnish SCHOOL BOARD's Contract Administrator with written verification of liability protection in accordance with state law prior to final execution of said Agreement.

7.3   COUNTY shall protect the property of SCHOOL BOARD by following the same or similar procedures used to protect the COUNTY's library property. However, COUNTY shall not be liable to SCHOOL BOARD for loss or damage to any of SCHOOL BOARD's property, except as otherwise set forth in Article 6, Section 6.2 above.

7.4   Property of SCHOOL BOARD which becomes worn or damaged and is no longer useful for its intended purpose may be disposed of by COUNTY in the same or similar manner used to dispose of COUNTY's library property which becomes worn or damaged and is no longer useful, however, in no event shall disposal occur without the prior written approval of SCHOOL BOARD"S representative.

7.5   The parties agree that the obligations under this Article shall survive the expiration or termination of this Agreement and shall remain in full force and effect notwithstanding the formal expiration or termination of this Agreement.

ARTICLE 8

TERMINATION

8.1   This Agreement may be terminated for cause by action of COUNTY, through action of its Board or COUNTY's Contract Administrator, upon not less than five (5) days' written notice by its Contract Administrator. This Agreement may be terminated for cause by action of SCHOOL BOARD, through action of its Board or Contract Administrator, upon not less than five (5) days' written notice by its Contract Administrator to SCHOOL BOARD.

8.2   This Agreement may be terminated for convenience by COUNTY, through action of its Board, upon not less than thirty (30) days' written notice by COUNTY's Contract Administrator. This Agreement may be terminated for convenience by SCHOOL BOARD, through action of its Board, upon not less than thirty (30) days' written notice by SCHOOL BOARD's Contract Administrator to COUNTY.

8.3   Termination of this Agreement for cause shall include, but not be limited to, failure of COUNTY or SCHOOL BOARD to suitably perform its scope of services; failure of COUNTY or SCHOOL BOARD to continuously perform the work in a manner calculated to meet or accomplish the objectives of COUNTY and SCHOOL BOARD as set forth in this Agreement; failure of SCHOOL BOARD to pay invoices submitted in a timely manner; failure of COUNTY or SCHOOL BOARD to perform its obligation under the Agreement; or multiple breach of the provisions of this Agreement notwithstanding whether any such breach was previously waived or cured.

8.4   Notice of termination shall be provided in accordance with the "NOTICES" section set forth in Article 9, Section 9.8 of this Agreement.

8.5   In the event this Agreement is terminated by either party for convenience, COUNTY shall be paid for any services performed to the date the Agreement is terminated; however, upon being notified of SCHOOL BOARD's election to terminate, COUNTY shall refrain from performing further services or incurring additional expenses under the terms of this Agreement. SCHOOL BOARD and COUNTY acknowledge and agree that ten dollars ($10.00) of the compensation to be paid by them, the adequacy of which is hereby acknowledged by each party, is given as specific consideration to the other party for each party's right to terminate this Agreement for convenience.

ARTICLE 9

MISCELLANEOUS

9.1   OWNERSHIP OF DOCUMENTS

Any and all reports, photographs, surveys, and other data and documents provided or created by COUNTY in connection with this Agreement are and shall remain the property of COUNTY. In the event of termination of this Agreement, any reports, photographs, surveys, and other data and documents prepared by COUNTY, whether finished or unfinished, shall become the property of COUNTY and shall be delivered by SCHOOL BOARD to the Contract Administrator.

9.2   AUDIT RIGHT AND RETENTION OF RECORDS

SCHOOL BOARD shall have the right to audit the books, records, and accounts of COUNTY. COUNTY shall keep such books, records, and accounts as may be necessary in order to record complete and correct entries related to the Project.

COUNTY shall preserve and make available, at reasonable times for examination and audit by SCHOOL BOARD, all financial records, supporting documents, statistical records, and any other documents pertinent to this Agreement for the required retention period of the Florida Public Records Act (Chapter 119, Fla. Stat.), if applicable, or, if the Florida Public Records Act is not applicable, for a minimum period of three (3) years after final payments are made or three (3) years after termination of this Agreement, whichever is later. If any audit has been initiated and audit findings have not been resolved at the end of the retention period or three (3) years, whichever is longer, the books, records, and accounts shall be retained until resolution of the audit findings.

The Florida Public Records Act is determined by COUNTY and SCHOOL BOARD to be applicable to COUNTY's records, COUNTY and SCHOOL BOARD shall comply with all requirements thereof; however, no confidentiality or non-disclosure requirement of either federal or state law shall be violated by COUNTY and SCHOOL BOARD.

COUNTY shall grant to SCHOOL BOARD, the Federal Grantor, the Comptroller General of the United States, the State Auditor General, or any of their duly authorized representatives access to any books, documents, papers, and records belonging to either party pertinent to this contract.

9.3   PUBLIC ENTITY CRIMES ACT

COUNTY and SCHOOL BOARD represent to each other that the individual party's respective execution of this Agreement will not violate the Public Entity Crimes Act (Section 287.133, Florida Statutes), which essentially provides that a person or affiliate who is a contractor, consultant or other provider and who has been placed on the convicted vendor list following a conviction for a Public Entity Crime may not submit a bid on a contract to provide any goods or services to COUNTY or SCHOOL BOARD, may not submit a bid on a contract with COUNTY or SCHOOL BOARD for the construction or repair of a public building or public work, may not submit bids on leases of real property to COUNTY or SCHOOL BOARD, may not be awarded or perform work as a contractor, supplier, subcontractor, or consultant under a contract with COUNTY or SCHOOL BOARD, and may not transact any business with COUNTY or SCHOOL BOARD in excess of the threshold amount provided in Section 287.017, Florida Statutes, for category two purchases for a period of 36 months from the date of being placed on the convicted vendor list. Violation of this section shall result in termination of this Agreement and recovery of all monies paid or expenses incurred hereto, and may result in debarment from COUNTY's and SCHOOL BOARD's competitive procurement activities.

In addition to the foregoing, COUNTY and SCHOOL BOARD further represent to each other that there has been no determination, based on an audit, that it committed an act defined by Section 287.133, Florida Statutes, as a "public entity crime" and that it has not been formally charged with committing an act defined as a "public entity crime" regardless of the amount of money involved or whether COUNTY or SCHOOL BOARD have been placed on the convicted vendor list.

9.4   INDEPENDENT CONTRACTOR

COUNTY and SCHOOL BOARD are independent contractors under this Agreement. Services provided by each party shall be subject to the supervision of the party providing the service. The parties expressly acknowledge that it is not their intent to create any rights or obligations in any third person or entity under this Agreement.

9.5   PRIOR AGREEMENTS

This document incorporates and includes all prior negotiations, correspondence, conversations, agreements, and understandings applicable to the matters contained herein and the parties agree that there are no commitments, agreements or understandings concerning the subject matter of this Agreement that are not contained in this document. Accordingly, the parties agree that no deviation from the terms hereof shall be predicated upon any prior representations or agreements, whether oral or written. It is further agreed that no modification, amendment or alteration in the terms or conditions contained herein shall be effective unless contained in a written document in accordance with Section 9.18 below. The COUNTY and the SCHOOL BOARD agree that the parties' agreement concerning the Pembroke Pines Joint Middle School/Public Library Branch remains in full force and effect and is not incorporated into or made a part of this document since the parties already have a very specific and separate agreement concerning that branch.

9.6 THIRD PARTY BENEFICIARIES

Neither COUNTY nor SCHOOL BOARD intends to directly or substantially benefit a third party by this Agreement. Therefore, the parties agree that there are no third party beneficiaries to this Agreement and that no third party shall be entitled to assert a claim against either of them based upon this Agreement.

9.7 NOTICES

Whenever either party desires to give notice to the other, such notice must be in writing, sent by certified United States Mail, postage prepaid, return receipt requested, or by hand-delivery with a request for a written receipt of acknowledgment of delivery, addressed to the party for whom it is intended at the place last specified. The place for giving notice shall remain the same as set forth herein until changed in writing in the manner provided in this section. For the present, the parties designate the following:

FOR BROWARD COUNTY:

FOR SCHOOL BOARD:

9.8 ASSIGNMENT AND PERFORMANCE

Neither this Agreement nor any interest herein shall be assigned, transferred, or encumbered by either party and neither party shall not subcontract any portion of the work required by this Agreement.

COUNTY and SCHOOL BOARD represents that all persons delivering the services required by this Agreement have the knowledge and skills, either by training, experience, education, or a combination thereof, to adequately and competently perform the duties, obligations, and services set forth in the Scope of Services and to provide and perform such services to the satisfaction of both parties for the agreed compensation.

COUNTY and SCHOOL BOARD shall perform its duties, obligations, and services under this Agreement in a skillful and respectable manner. The quality of each party's performance and all interim and final product(s) provided to or on behalf of either party shall be comparable to the best local and national standards.

9.9 CONFLICTS

COUNTY and SCHOOL BOARD agree that neither party nor any of its employees shall, during the term of this Agreement, have or hold any continuing or frequently recurring employment or contractual relationship that is substantially antagonistic or incompatible with the party's loyal and conscientious exercise of judgment related to its performance under this Agreement.

COUNTY and SCHOOL BOARD agree that neither party nor any of its employees shall, during the term of this Agreement, serve as an adverse or hostile witness against the other party in any legal or administrative proceeding in which it is not a party, unless compelled by court process, nor shall such persons give sworn testimony or issue a report or writing, as an expression of its opinion, which is adverse or prejudicial to the interests of the other party in any such pending or threatened legal or administrative proceeding. The limitations of this section shall not preclude such persons from representing themselves in any action or in any administrative or legal proceeding regarding this Agreement.

In the event COUNTY and SCHOOL BOARD are permitted to utilize subcontractors to perform any services required by this Agreement, each party agrees to prohibit such subcontractors, by written contract, from having any conflicts as within the meaning of this section.

9.10 CONTINGENCY FEE

COUNTY and SCHOOL BOARD warrant that they have not employed or retained any company or person, other than a bona fide employee working solely for the respective party, to solicit or secure this Agreement and that it has not paid or agreed to pay any person, company, corporation, individual or firm, other than a bona fide employee working solely for the respective party, any fee, commission, percentage, gift, or other consideration contingent upon or resulting from the award or making of this Agreement. For a breach or violation of this provision, the other party shall have the right to terminate this Agreement without liability at its discretion, or to deduct from the Agreement price or otherwise recover the full amount of such fee, commission, percentage, gift or consideration.

9.11   COMPLIANCE WITH LAWS

COUNTY and SCHOOL BOARD shall comply with all federal, state, and local laws, codes, ordinances, rules, and regulations in performing its duties, responsibilities, and obligations related to this Agreement.

9.12   SEVERANCE

In the event this Agreement or a portion of this Agreement is found by a court of competent jurisdiction to be invalid, the remaining provisions shall continue to be effective unless COUNTY or SCHOOL BOARD elects to terminate this Agreement. The election to terminate this Agreement based upon this provision shall be made within seven (7) days after the finding by the court becomes final.

9.13   JOINT PREPARATION

Preparation of this Agreement has been a joint effort of COUNTY and SCHOOL BOARD and the resulting document shall not, solely as a matter of judicial construction, be construed more severely against one of the parties than any other.

9.14   PRIORITY OF PROVISIONS

If there is a conflict or inconsistency between any term, statement, requirement, or provision of any exhibit attached hereto, any document or events referred to herein, or any document incorporated into this Agreement by reference and a term, statement, requirement, or provision of this Agreement, the term, statement, requirement, or provision contained in Articles 1 through 9 of this Agreement shall prevail and be given effect.

9.15   CLAIMS; APPLICABLE LAW AND VENUE

The parties agree that resolution of the dispute excluding funding disputes will be determined by a majority vote of a committee consisting of: Director of Broward County Libraries Division; Associate Superintendent of Accountability, Technology, Strategic Planning and School Improvement; Director of Main Library; Director of Exceptional Student Education; Coordinator of Florida Diagnostic and Learning Resources Systems (FDLRS); and the Director of Learning Resources.

This Agreement shall be interpreted and construed in accordance with and governed by the laws of the State of Florida. Venue for litigation concerning this Agreement shall be in Broward County, Florida.

9.15   AMENDMENTS

No modification, amendment, or alteration in the terms or conditions contained herein shall be effective unless contained in a written document prepared with the same or similar formality as this Agreement and executed by COUNTY, through action of its Board, and by SCHOOL BOARD.

9.16   INCORPORATION BY REFERENCE

The truth and accuracy of each "Whereas" clause set forth above is acknowledged by the parties.

IN WITNESS WHEREOF, the parties hereto have made and executed this Agreement: BROWARD COUNTY through its BOARD OF COUNTY COMMISSIONERS, signing by and through its Chair or Vice Chair, authorized to execute same by Board action on the _____ day of _____, 19____, and SCHOOL BOARD, signing by and through its _____, duly authorized to execute same.

Contributors

Shirley Amore Director, Sarasota County Libraries, formerly associate director for central services at Main Library, Broward County Library. Ms. Amore brings with her extensive experience in public/private partnerships involving libraries.

Jerrie Bethel Librarian at The Freedom Forum, a media foundation, and Newseum, a news museum, in Arlington, Virginia. After earning her B.S. in print journalism from Florida International University, she acquired an M.L.S. from University of South Florida, while working as a children's librarian at Broward County Library.

Joann Block Access Services and Talking Book Coordinator, Broward County Library. She received her M.L.S. from Pratt Institute, and is currently working on a doctorate in adult education/human resource development at Florida International University.

Elizabeth Curry Executive Director of SEFLIN since 1991. Prior to working with SEFLIN she was the marketing manager for SOLINET and spent three years at the State Library of Florida as a library development consultant. Ms. Curry began her career with the DeKalb County Public Library System, Georgia, with positions including training coordinator, community services & public relations coordinator and planning & development coordinator.

Cynthia Genovese-Shulman FDLRS Media Center Coordinator, Broward County Library since 1992. She has also had responsibility for the School Professional Collection since 1995. Ms. Genovese-Shulman received a B.S. in education from the University of Michigan and taught at the preschool level for several years. Following a Peace Corps assignment in Botswana, she came to Broward County, serving also as Volunteer Coordinator for the library.

Marlene Lee Youth Services Coordinator, Broward County Library since 1990, and a children's librarian for almost 25 years. Ms. Lee graduated from Slippery Rock University (PA) with a degree in secondary education and received her M.L.S. from the University of South Florida in 1983.

Sherry Lynch Assistant Director, Community Relations & Partnership Development, Broward County Library. She is a graduate of the University of Idaho and holds a masters degree in public administration from Mississippi State University. She has worked for Broward County government since 1981, serving as a special assistant to the county administrator and as a budget analyst prior to joining the library staff in 1985.

Mary McBride Vice President for Broward Campuses, Florida Atlantic University. She came to FAU in 1990 as dean of the College of Liberal Arts, and has served as vice president since 1992. Dr. McBride is responsible for initiating and nurturing partnerships for the university in Broward County.

Jennifer Carrigan Morrison South Area Coordinator for Palm Beach County Library System. She served as a branch librarian at Broward County's Fort Lauderdale Branch Library for four years, working through the planning, renovation, re-opening, and cooperative operations of the branch with its partner ArtServe. Ms. Morrison has a M.L.S. from the University of South Florida.

Samuel F. Morrison Director of the Broward County Library System since 1990. He served as the chief librarian for the City of Chicago from April 1987 to January 1990. During that time he was responsible for the planning, design, and initial construction phases of the new Harold Washington Library Center. Prior to his stint in Chicago, he had served as the deputy directory of the Broward County Library System from August 1974 to April 1987. Mr. Morrison, while serving as president of the Southeast Florida Library Information Network, was instrumental in developing and implementing the SEFLIN Free-Net.

Debbie Passalacqua Regional Supervisor, Broward County Library. She administers the North Regional/BCC Library and supervises branches in the northern area of Broward County. In addition to joint-use libraries, she also has a special interest in library services to deaf people and helped develop the first American guidelines for library services to the deaf community. She is an active lecturer on both topics and enjoys meeting the many people across the country involved in either endeavor.

Tanya Simons-Oparah Assistant Director, Outreach Services, Broward County Library since 1988. She has been with Broward County Library for over twenty years developing programs and services in staff development, distance learning and services to new and underserved community members.

Jean Trebbi Executive Director, Florida Center for the Book. Ms. Trebbi received her M.L.S. from Rutgers and has worked as a librarian for over twenty years with Broward County in both reference and special collections.

Index